FEARLESS
LIVING

IN TROUBLED TIMES

MICHAEL YOUSSEF

HARVEST HOUSE PUBLISHERS
EUGENE, OREGON

Unless otherwise indicated, all Scripture quotations are from the Holy Bible, New International Version®, NIV®. Copyright © 1973, 1978, 1984, 2011 by Biblica, Inc.® Used by permission. All rights reserved worldwide.

Verses marked KJV are taken from the King James Version of the Bible.

Cover by Brian Bobel Design, Whites Creek, TN

Cover Image © olgaIT / iStock

Published in association with Don Gates of the literary agency The Gates Group, www.the-gates-group.com.

FEARLESS LIVING IN TROUBLED TIMES
Copyright © 2017 Michael Youssef
Published by Harvest House Publishers
Eugene, Oregon 97402
www.harvesthousepublishers.com

ISBN 978-0-7369-6802-7 (pbk.)
ISBN 978-0-7369-6803-4 (eBook)

Library of Congress Cataloging-in-Publication Data
Names: Youssef, Michael, author.
Title: Fearless living in troubled times : finding hope in the promise of
   Christ's return / Michael Youssef.
Description: Eugene, Oregon : Harvest House Publishers, 2017. | Description
   based on print version record and CIP data provided by publisher; resource
   not viewed.
Identifiers: LCCN 2017001284 (print) | LCCN 2017015668 (ebook) | ISBN
   9780736968034 (ebook) | ISBN 9780736968027 (pbk.)
Subjects: LCSH: Bible. Thessalonians—Commentaries.
Classification: LCC BS2725.53 (ebook) | LCC BS2725.53 .Y68 2017 (print) | DDC
   227/.8107—dc23
LC record available at https://lccn.loc.gov/2017001284

All rights reserved. No part of this publication may be reproduced, stored in a retrieval system, or transmitted in any form or by any means—electronic, mechanical, digital, photocopy, recording, or any other—except for brief quotations in printed reviews, without the prior permission of the publisher.

Printed in the United States of America

17 18 19 20 21 22 23 24 25 / BP-SK / 10 9 8 7 6 5 4 3 2

To Rick and Andee Swanson,
in deep gratitude to God for
their faithfulness and true partnership
in the gospel of Jesus Christ
around the world

Acknowledgments

I am thankful to God for giving me the privilege of writing this exploration of the great themes of 1 and 2 Thessalonians.

I'm also grateful to the Lord for sending me an able editor and compiler of my material in Jim Denney.

Special thanks to the entire team at Harvest House Publishers, who shared my vision and made this dream a reality. Thanks also to Donald W. Gates Jr., founder and principal of the Gates Group, for managing the many details of this project.

I pray that, as I leave this legacy to the next generation, God would raise up a new generation of faithful men and women who would accurately interpret the living Word of God.

Contents

LIVING FAITHFULLY, LIVING FEARLESSLY

We live in an age of fear, an age that seems poised for the apocalypse.

Rogue nations are going nuclear. Terrorists and jihadists are springing up in our midst, committing senseless mass murders in once-safe cities like Orlando and San Bernardino. Across North Africa and the Middle East, terrorists commit beheadings and other atrocities, then post video of these acts on the Internet to shock the world. Wars ignite across the globe, and rumors of wars spread like wildfire. Fears of climate change are mounting. Resources are dwindling. Strange new diseases are mutating and threatening our children. Racial tensions have led us to the precipice of a race war. The national debt keeps rising, and there is no political will to stop it—which means that a global economic collapse is just a matter of time.

In the midst of all these threats, we find ourselves living in a post-Christian age, when all of our beliefs and values are under attack from a hostile media, the government, and even our neighbors and coworkers. Yes, we live in an age of fear, a climate of suspense. It's as if the entire world is waiting for Something Big to happen—something terrifying and apocalyptic. In May 2016, the highly respected British daily, *The Guardian*, published a report on the deepening fear and anxiety throughout our culture:

We live with an epidemic of anxiety. In 1980, 4 percent of Americans suffered a mental disorder associated with anxiety. Today half do. The trends in Britain are similar. A third of Britons will experience anxiety disorder at some stage in their life, with an explosion of reported anxiety among teenagers and young adults. Anxiety, depression, self-harm, attention deficit disorder and profound eating problems afflict our young as never before.

Anxiety has always been part of the human condition—as has depression and tendencies to self-harm—but never, it seems, on this scale. A number of trends appear to be colliding. This is an era when everyone is expected to find their personal route to happiness at the same time as the bonds of society, faith and community—tried and tested mechanisms to support wellbeing—are fraying. Teenagers in particular—fearful of missing out—are beset by a myriad of agonizing choices about how to achieve the good life with fewer social and psychological anchors to help them navigate their way. Who can blame them if they respond with an ever rising sense of anxiety, if not panic?[1]

The Guardian concludes that this mood of spreading fear is due to a "fraying" of "the bonds of society, faith and community." We are witnessing the collapse of the family, social structure, and the community, with the result that people feel increasingly vulnerable and fearful.

But God does not want his people to be anxious or afraid. For believers like you and me, these times are reminiscent of another time in history. In spite of superficial differences of supersonic travel, high-tech media, and the Internet, the twenty-first-century world exhibits many surprising parallels to the first-century world of the New Testament writers.

Fear was rampant in the first century. Crime, terrorism, plagues, famines, and wars were a constant fact of life in that era. Political oppression was the order of the day throughout the iron-fisted Roman empire. Christians in the first century were specially singled out for persecution—which often involved the arrest of entire families, followed by horrifying tortures and martyrdom. Those were troubled times, and Paul wrote two letters of encouragement to the church he founded in Thessalonica during his second missionary journey—encouragement to live faithfully and fearlessly in the midst of those dangerous times.

The Greek city of Thessalonica was ancient even in Paul's day, having been founded around 315 BC by King Cassander of Macedon. He named it after his wife Thessalonike, the half-sister of Alexander the Great. The Thessalonian believers were a model of faithfulness, living in a culturally important city with a substantial population of Hellenized Jews (that is, Jews who had been culturally influenced by the Greeks).

Acts 17 tells the story of how Paul founded the Thessalonian church—and how he escaped being murdered by an angry Thessalonian mob:

> When Paul and his companions had passed through Amphipolis and Apollonia, they came to Thessalonica, where there was a Jewish synagogue. As was his custom, Paul went into the synagogue, and on three Sabbath days he reasoned with them from the Scriptures, explaining and proving that the Messiah had to suffer and rise from the dead. "This Jesus I am proclaiming to you is the Messiah," he said. Some of the Jews were persuaded and joined Paul and Silas, as did a large number of God-fearing Greeks and quite a few prominent women.
>
> But other Jews were jealous; so they rounded up some bad characters from the marketplace, formed a mob and started a riot in the city. They rushed to Jason's house in search of Paul and Silas in order to bring them out to the crowd. But when they did not find them, they dragged Jason and some other believers before the city officials, shouting: "These men who have caused trouble all over the world have now come here, and Jason has welcomed them into his house.

They are all defying Caesar's decrees, saying that there is another king, one called Jesus." When they heard this, the crowd and the city officials were thrown into turmoil. Then they made Jason and the others post bond and let them go.

As soon as it was night, the believers sent Paul and Silas away to Berea. On arriving there, they went to the Jewish synagogue...But when the Jews in Thessalonica learned that Paul was preaching the word of God at Berea, some of them went there too, agitating the crowds and stirring them up (Acts 17:1-10,13).

As is often the case, those who hated the gospel persecuted the messenger. They wanted to kill Paul, but he got out of Thessalonica just in time. He left behind many faithful believers, and it broke his heart. He dearly loved the Thessalonians who had received the gospel of Jesus Christ with joy and sincerity. He looked forward to returning to Thessalonica to spend more time with them and to help establish them in the faith.

Paul wrote 1 Thessalonians in AD 51 or 52, and it was probably the first of all Paul's letters to the churches (though some Bible scholars think Galatians might have been written before 1 Thessalonians). If 1 Thessalonians was written first, it would be the oldest book in the New Testament. Paul's next letter, 2 Thessalonians, was probably written within a few months of the first.

Paul's reasons for writing these two letters include: encouraging the church, refuting false allegations, comforting the persecuted believers, encouraging them to maintain their moral purity, correcting misinformation and false teachings about prophetic events, and teaching the basics of living a fearless Christian life in the midst of a disintegrating society.

So these two letters serve as a unified message of instruction on a number of issues:

- how to build and maintain a healthy church
- the importance of evangelism and church planting

- the value of godly living and morality
- the necessity of living productively and supporting one's family
- above all, the great theological questions surrounding the second coming of Christ

Paul wrote these letters to a church that was enduring troubled times. His words sent a message of faith and fearlessness to the Thessalonians, and to you and me—a message that points to the ultimate hope of all believers, the blessed return of our Lord Jesus Christ.

THE END-TIMES PARADOX

1 Thessalonians 1

S ome time ago, a radio broadcaster announced that the Lord Jesus would return to earth on May 21, 2011, to take his followers out of the world and set in motion the terrifying events of the great tribulation. Many people sold their possessions and emptied their bank accounts to fund a $100 million evangelistic campaign based on that prediction.

One young engineer at a Fortune 500 company quit the job he loved because he was certain the world was ending. In his resignation letter, he told his employer, "I desire to spend more time studying the Bible and sounding the trumpet warning of this imminent judgment."

Another man with a good job cashed out his retirement savings—more than half a million dollars—and bought an RV that he had custom-painted with Bible verses and end-of-the-world warnings. He used the rest of his savings to buy full-page newspaper ads warning that the rapture would occur on May 21.

The night before the big day, many believers stayed up all night, watching CNN or checking Google News on their computers, expecting reports of a massive earthquake that they believed would herald the second coming. Others went to bed as usual, expecting to awaken in heaven. But the red-letter date came and went—and the world went on unchanged. Those who had fallen for the false prediction—and especially those who lost everything they owned because of it—felt duped, disillusioned, and angry. Some even turned their backs on the Christian faith.

One man, a father of three, told a reporter, "You know what? I think I was part of a cult." His biggest concern was how his sons, all of whom were old enough to understand, would look back on a failed prediction that the whole family had bought into. How would this event affect their faith in God and their view of their parents? "When my kids are older," he said, "they're going to say that we're the crazy parents who believed the world was going to end."[2]

It's tragic when a false prophecy, based largely on human reasoning and wishful thinking, brings discredit and derision on God's prophetic Word. When human illusions about Bible prophecy are exposed, the result is disillusionment. A misplaced belief in one man's word often undermines belief in God's Word.

Fortunately, most mainstream evangelicals put no stock in this radio broadcaster's prediction. Christians today continue to be fascinated with prophecies of the end times. Many Christians are convinced, with good reason, that we might well be the last generation on earth. A 2014 Reuters poll found that almost a quarter of all Americans and one-seventh of the people of the world expect to see the end of the world in their lifetime.[3] There has never been more interest in the end times than there is right now.

It's perfectly right and fitting that we, as God's people, should be attentive to Bible prophecy. After all, a major portion of God's Word is devoted to prophecy. According to J. Barton Payne's *Encyclopedia of Biblical Prophecy*, 8352 of the Bible's 31,124 verses (almost 27 percent!) are devoted to Bible prophecy.[4] So God clearly wants us to understand the basic outline of his plan for human history, which he has revealed to us in Bible prophecy.

Unfortunately, many Christians have taken a godly interest in Bible prophecy to ungodly extremes—including the arrogant extreme of pretending to know the exact date of the Lord's return. Jesus himself warned against such foolishness, saying, "But about that day or hour no one knows, not even the angels in heaven, nor the Son, but only the Father" (Matthew 24:36). That warning hasn't stopped certain TV preachers and authors who pretend to possess hidden knowledge of God's timetable. Like the man who predicted the end of the world in 2011, they always have a reasonable-sounding explanation for why the Lord's warning doesn't apply to *them*.

The Bible encourages us to study its prophetic passages—but the Bible also warns us not to become obsessed with predicting the dates and times. It's not our job to know exactly when any given event will take place. Our job is to preach the good news and to be spiritually and morally ready at all times for the Lord's return.

There's a strange paradox taking place in the church today, and it is focused on Bible prophecy. I call it the end-times paradox. The paradox is simply this: There has never been more interest in the end times than there is today—yet that interest is not being manifested in the lives of Christians.

For example, the Left Behind series is a franchise of sixteen best-selling novels that fictionalize a dispensationalist version of the end times. Published from 1995 to 2007, with many spinoffs, adaptations, and merchandise, including movies and video games, the Left Behind series has earned hundreds of millions of dollars for its publisher, Tyndale House, prompting one critic in *Vanity Fair* to label the series "the new wave of Rapturemania."[5] As you might expect, sales of Left Behind books and merchandise were driven by Christians—yet Christians give less than 2.6 percent of their income to the church (incredibly, Christians are less generous in these prosperous times than they were during the Great Depression, when Christians gave an average of 3.3 percent of their income).

Prophecy conferences with speakers and authors promoting their end-times merchandise easily draw tens of thousands of people—yet prayer meetings draw very few. Social media is abuzz with various theories about the rapture (the return of Christ for his church), the signs of the great tribulation, and the identity of the antichrist—yet fewer and fewer Christians are willing to witness for their faith.

Do you see the paradox? How can anyone sincerely await the return of the Lord, yet live as if the world will go on forever? How can we be watching for the second coming—yet we do so little to reach out to those who would be left behind? There's nothing wrong with reading about the end times and learning about Bible prophecy, but shouldn't we also spend time inviting the lost into the Lord's kingdom?

One day, the Lord will return to take us to heaven. This truth ought to motivate every dimension of our lives. It ought to inspire us to serve more, to witness more, to give more, to pray more, and to live in the daily expectation that Christ could return at any moment.

C.S. Lewis once made this convicting statement:

> If you read history, you will find that the Christians who did most for the present world were just those who thought most of the next. The Apostles themselves, who set on foot the conversion of the Roman Empire, the great men who built up the Middle Ages, the English Evangelicals who abolished the Slave Trade, all left their mark on Earth, pre-cisely because their minds were occupied with Heaven. It is since Christians have largely ceased to think of the other world that they have become so ineffective in this. Aim at Heaven and you will get earth "thrown in:" aim at earth and you will get neither.[6]

In 2006 the Pew Research Center found that 79 percent of Christians believe in the return of Christ, and 20 percent believe that the Lord Jesus will return in their lifetime.[7] You'd think that these beliefs would be translated into meaningful, visible action. You'd think that people would behave more selflessly, witness more fervently, give more generously.

Our generation is not the only generation that has strongly believed in the imminent return of Christ. From the early church to the present day, believers have had a compelling fascination with the *Parousia* (a theological term referring to the Lord's return to take believers to heaven, from an ancient Greek word meaning "arrival" or "official visit"). That's why the apostle Paul, writing to the Thessalonians, was eager to dispel the many false and confused notions people had about the *Parousia*. He made it clear to the Thessalonian believers, who were living in troubled times, that they should live expectantly, eagerly awaiting the return of Christ—and that meant they must live as though Christ might return any day, at any moment.

In short, if we say we expect the return of Christ at any time, we should live like it. And Paul spends the first half of 1 Thessalonians explaining how a Christian awaiting the return of Christ should live. In the second half of 1 Thessalonians, he explains what will take place when the Lord returns to earth.

A WORKING FAITH, AN ACTIVE FAITH

The apostle Paul, writing under the inspiration of the Holy Spirit, begins this magnificent letter by thanking God for the powerful Christian witness of the Thessalonian believers:

> Paul, Silas and Timothy,
>
> To the church of the Thessalonians in God the Father and the Lord Jesus Christ:
>
> Grace and peace to you.
>
> We always thank God for all of you and continually mention you in our prayers. We remember before our God and Father your work produced by faith, your labor prompted by love, and your endurance inspired by hope in our Lord Jesus Christ.
>
> For we know, brothers and sisters loved by God, that he has chosen you, because our gospel came to you not simply with words but also with power, with the Holy Spirit and deep conviction. You know how we lived among you for your sake. You became imitators of us and of the Lord, for you welcomed the message in the midst of severe suffering with the joy given by the Holy Spirit. And so you became a model to all the believers in Macedonia and Achaia. The Lord's message rang out from you not only in Macedonia and Achaia—your faith in God has become known everywhere. Therefore we do not need to say anything about it,

for they themselves report what kind of reception you gave us. They tell how you turned to God from idols to serve the living and true God, and to wait for his Son from heaven, whom he raised from the dead—Jesus, who rescues us from the coming wrath (1 Thessalonians 1:1-10).

In these opening verses, Paul describes ten distinctive traits of the Thessalonian believers: (1) They had a working faith, (2) they had a laboring love, (3) they exhibited an enduring hope, (4) they displayed humility before God for his election and power, (5) they were genuine imitators of Christ, (6) they had joy in the midst of trouble, (7) they lived exemplary lives, (8) they had zeal in their witnessing, (9) they demonstrated transformed lives, and (10) they expectantly awaited the return of the Lord Jesus. To summarize, Paul said that the Thessalonian believers were characterized by faith, love, and hope—the three indispensable traits of a genuine Christian.

Each of these traits is outgoing, not inward; active, not passive; visible, not hidden; public, not private. Faith is active toward God. Love is active toward other people. Hope is active toward our expectation of the Lord's return.

Faith is anchored in the past, in actual historic events, as we look back to the Lord's saving work on the cross. Love is anchored in the present, as we practice Christlike love toward the people around us. Hope is anchored in the future, in the trustworthy promises God gave us in his Word.

Every genuine Christian trusts in God's Word, puts his or her beliefs into action toward others, and is confident of his or her ultimate destination. These three traits—faith, love, and hope—prove that we follow Christ, not just on Sunday but every day of the week.

Some people say, "I have faith, but I like to keep my faith private." Biblically, that's nonsense. The Bible does not recognize a "private" faith. Faith is, by definition, visible and active. Faith must work. Love must labor. Hope must endure.

Faith in the Lord Jesus Christ—his death and resurrection—is our only means of salvation. Our faith must always be a working faith, an active faith, not a dead faith because a dead or inactive faith is not faith at all. The apostle James tells us:

> What good is it, my brothers and sisters, if someone claims to have faith but has no deeds? Can such faith save them? Suppose a brother or a sister is without clothes and daily food. If one of you says to them, "Go in peace; keep warm and well fed," but does nothing about their physical needs, what good is it? In the same way, faith by itself, if it is not accompanied by action, is dead.
>
> But someone will say, "You have faith; I have deeds."
>
> Show me your faith without deeds, and I will show you my faith by my deeds (James 2:14-18).

If anyone claims to have faith, that faith will be manifested through visible acts of serving, witnessing, and giving. True faith will be expressed in love.

Authentic Christian love is exhibited through labor. What kind of labor? The labor of sacrificing. The labor of forgiving. The labor of persevering. The labor of stretching oneself out to the very limits of endurance in service to God and others. Any so-called "love" that does not labor is mere sentimentality.

True hope waits patiently, and it works as it waits. Authentic Christian hope is not demonstrated by putting on white robes, climbing to a mountaintop, and saying, "Take me away, Lord!" An authentic Christian hope is not expressed by hunkering down in a bunker and doing nothing. Hope is involved with the sufferings of humanity. Hope rolls up its sleeves and gets its hands dirty. Hope is continually lighting candles of faith in the hearts of others.

In times of persecution and oppression, hope endures. Hope perseveres. Hope brings us peace in the midst of trouble. The serene and confident expectation of the return of Jesus Christ, whether his return takes place in the next instant or ten thousand years from now, fills us with a peace that no persecutor can take away.

THE DYNAMITE OF THE GOSPEL

In 1 Thessalonians 1, Paul draws a correlation between the love of God and election, which is also known as predestination. God loves us, and God chose us. Why did he choose us? Was it because we are so lovable? Absolutely not! We were enemies of God by our very nature as children of Adam. Moreover, we were enemies of God by reason of our sinful and rebellious actions.

God chose us *not* because we are lovable but *in spite of* our unlovable condition. His love is unconditional. His choice was a function of his sovereign will. Why he chooses one and not another is a mystery known only to God. And because his sovereign election of you and me is an act of his sovereign grace, we have no reason to be arrogant. His election of us drives us to our knees in humility and brokenness before him.

We can only cry out to God and say, "Lord, I don't know why you love me, why you called me, why you chose me, why you predestined me—but in utter amazement and humility, I say thank you, I believe in you, and I want to spend all of eternity praising you." There is no power in the universe more humbling to our egos than the sovereign election of God.

Jesus said to his disciples, "You did not choose me, but I chose you and appointed you so that you might go and bear fruit—fruit that will last" (John 15:16a). If it were up to us, we would not choose to follow him. As fallen human beings, we are willful and rebellious by nature. Yet Paul says that God chose us so that we might make him known. "He has chosen you," Paul wrote, "because our gospel came to you not simply with words but also with power, with the Holy Spirit and deep conviction…You became imitators of us and of the Lord…The Lord's message rang out from you not only in Macedonia and Achaia—your faith in God has become known everywhere."

God chose us so that his message might ring out from us and the good news of Jesus Christ might become known everywhere. Paul shows us three stages by which the gospel progressed in Thessalonica: (1) the gospel came to the Thessalonians, (2) they welcomed its message, (3) and the message went out from the Thessalonians to the people round about them. This principle is stated again and again throughout Scripture: We are not saved merely for our own comfort and security. We are not saved in order that we would simply do nothing, say nothing, and allow the world to go to hell.

All too many people in the church today have an attitude that says, "I'm sure glad I'm saved. I'm sure glad my family is saved. Too bad about the rest of the world." Or, "I'm sure glad God chose me. But I'm not responsible for my neighbors, coworkers, or classmates." God didn't entrust his gospel to you so that you could hide it away. God saved you for a purpose. He placed you where you are for a purpose. He provided you with opportunities for a purpose.

Are you living up to the purpose God chose you to fulfill? Are you living up to his calling on your life? The gospel is communicated in words—but it is so much more than just words. The good news of Jesus Christ is *power*. It is dynamite. And I don't mean that in the flippant way. In Romans 1:16, Paul says that the gospel is "the power of God that brings salvation to everyone who believes." That word "power" is *dynamis* in the original Greek—the word from which we get our English word *dynamite*. So it is not stretching the meaning of God's Word to say that the gospel is the "dynamite" of God. It blasts through our sin and rebellion, our brokenness and fallenness, our objections and rejection, and it powerfully draws us to him.

Why does God need to dynamite people with the gospel? Because blind eyes will not be opened by mere words. Hard hearts will not be softened by mere words. Stubborn wills will not be broken by mere words. That is why the Holy Spirit must dynamite our souls and spirits and consciences with the dynamic power of the gospel.

I could speak the most eloquent words. I could offer the most compelling arguments. I could communicate with unparalleled passion and intensity. But until the Holy Spirit of God takes those words and infuses them with power, they will never open deaf ears or blind eyes. That is why our witnessing and our ministry to the world must be bathed in prayer. We dare not do or say anything without calling upon God's dynamite power.

In 1988, we began a small Atlanta-based radio ministry called Leading

The Way. It grew to become a global ministry, blanketing the world with the good news. One of the great privileges this ministry has given me is that I get to hear story after story of lives changed by the Word of God, especially in the Muslim world. I recently heard about a young Libyan man—I'll call him Shahid. He told us that he had studied the Islamic religion from age five to twenty. He had memorized the entire Qur'an and studied the prophetic hadiths (traditions) and the Sharia law. When he had questions and doubts about the Qur'an, the religious scholars told him not to think about his doubts, not to question his beliefs.

He went through four years of mental and spiritual struggle—an intense crisis of belief. Finally, he decided that the Islamic religion was not the truth. By a series of unlikely circumstances, he came in contact with our 24/7 TV channel we call THE KINGDOM SAT, which Leading The Way launched in 2009 to broadcast the gospel into the Muslim world. Amazed to find a Christian TV channel, he watched it day after day. He contacted our counselors and eventually traveled to Jordan for three months to study the Bible. Then he moved back to Libya, planning to be a witness for God there.

Soon after Shahid returned to his home country, our counselors lost contact with him. He stopped writing, and our counselors feared the worst. We later found out that Shahid had told his father he was a Christian, and his father became enraged and reported him to the Libyan government. The Libyan government ejected Shahid from the country, and he soon found himself in a United Nations refugee camp in Turkey. There, Muslim refugees twice attempted to murder him.

When our counselors finally located Shahid, they asked him, "Why did the other refugees want to kill you?"

"I couldn't keep my mouth shut," Shahid said. "I had to share Jesus with them."

It's exciting to see God opening minds and touching hearts like Shahid's. When you see Middle Eastern Christians, including former Muslims like Shahid, coming to Christ and sharing the good news with exuberance and urgency, knowing they are likely to be persecuted and even killed for their witness, it makes you wonder, "Why am I afraid to witness in America? I'm not worried that anyone would try to kill me or harm me for my witness, yet I'm afraid to open my mouth and tell the world that Jesus is my Lord and Savior."

The believers in Thessalonica faced a similar situation to the believers in Libya and throughout the Middle East. They were living in the midst of great tribulation and persecution, yet they had received the good news. Knowing full well the dangers they faced, they took a bold stand for Christ. And so should we.

The Word of Truth, the gospel of Jesus Christ, always arouses hostility. The authentic gospel always challenges human pride. Have you ever been persecuted for the sake of Christ? Today many Christians are undergoing torture and imprisonment, losing their homes and families, being beaten and killed for no other reason than saying, "Jesus is Lord." You may never have experienced that ultimate degree of suffering and persecution for the gospel. But I hope you have experienced *some* persecution at *some* time.

This world is hostile to the good news of Jesus Christ. If you are vocal about your faith, if you are open about your witness, then you should have experienced some of this world's hostility to the gospel—some name-calling, some mocking and jeering on social media, some snide remarks or being shunned by people at school or work. If you have *never* experienced even a little ridicule for your Christian witness, you should ask yourself, "Am I not vocal enough? Am I not bold enough? Am I not brave enough? Am I ashamed of the gospel of Jesus Christ? Am I too timid and silent? Does anyone even know I'm a Christian?"

The reason many Christians today do not experience opposition or hostility from the world is that they do not preach the authentic gospel of Jesus Christ. The true gospel is offensive to the world. But many Christians walk on eggshells, avoiding any subject that might offend. They never speak of sin, hell, judgment, atonement, the cross, the resurrection, or the blood of Jesus. No wonder they never experience any persecution! They are so bland and timid that there is nothing about them that would offend anyone.

But the Thessalonians suffered persecution. They preached the gospel of Jesus Christ, not only on Sunday mornings but on weekdays, in the marketplaces and neighborhoods of that pagan city. They spoke the truth—and the truth made a lot of people mad. Are you like the Thes-salonian Christians? Do you speak the truth daily to the people around you? Has anyone ever gotten mad at you for the sake of the gospel?

WAITING AND SERVING GO HAND IN HAND

Someone once asked me, "Michael, do you ever get angry when peo-ple attack you personally and publicly?" I said, "No, I can answer you truthfully, I never become angry when an unbeliever attacks me because of the truth of the gospel."

It never surprises me or troubles me or hurts my feelings when a secularist or an atheist or someone from another religion criticizes me for preaching the truth of God's Word. What truly breaks my heart is not an unbeliever's hostility but *a believer's apathy*. Whenever you share the good news, some people will welcome it, and others will be hostile toward it. The hostility of the world should never catch us by surprise.

Paul said, "You became imitators of us and of the Lord, for you wel-comed the message in the midst of severe suffering with the joy given by the Holy Spirit" (verse 6). In spite of the hostility and persecution all around them, the Thessalonians welcomed the good news with the joy of the Holy Spirit. The same Holy Spirit gives power to our witness. He is at work in us as we witness, and he is at work in those we witness to. He gives power—dynamite—to our words, and he opens the eyes and ears of those who see and hear us.

Some of those who hear our witness will receive it with joy, and oth-ers will not. Some will even be angry. Don't be intimidated; don't be fearful. Share your faith boldly in the power of the Holy Spirit. Don't think you can be a witness for Christ in your own strength—let the Spirit of God speak through you.

One thing is clear about these Thessalonian believers: They did not sit on their blessed assurance after they came to Christ. They moved out, fearlessly and dynamically, and they impacted the world for Jesus. Paul writes, "The Lord's message rang out from you not only in Mace-donia and Achaia—your faith in God has become known everywhere" (verse 8). Wouldn't it be wonderful if such things were said of you and me? Wouldn't it be wonderful if our faith in God was known everywhere?

How does that kind of vibrant witness take place? It takes place when lives are completely transformed. Paul writes, "They tell how you turned to God from idols to serve the living and true God, and to wait for his Son from heaven, whom he raised from the dead—Jesus, who rescues us from the coming wrath" (verses 9b-10). The Thessalonians had been idol worshipers—but they had made a 180-degree turnabout. They had broken away from idols and now served the one true God. Not only did they serve God, but they patiently awaited the return of his Son, the risen Lord Jesus.

Here we see the three great evidences of faith: (1) You turn. (2) You serve. (3) You wait for Jesus to return.

You might say, "But Michael, I don't worship idols. I've never bowed down to an idol in my life. This passage doesn't apply to me."

Please understand, an idol is not merely a little god fashioned out of tin or stone. An idol is anything—or anyone—that occupies our attention, our finances, and our time. An idol is anything or anyone that controls us. An idol is anything that takes the place in our lives where God belongs. Our idols today might be selfish ambitions, or the accumulation of wealth and power, or an infatuation with another person, or an addiction to a substance or a behavior, or an obsession with pleasure and fun.

Many of us who claim Jesus as Lord and Savior would have to admit that these are idols in our lives. By the grace of God, by the power of the Holy Spirit, we need to declare that we hereby turn away from these idols, and we turn to the living God.

The Bible repeatedly contrasts idol worship versus faithfulness to God. Idols are dead; God is alive. Idols are false; God is the Truth. Idols are many; God is one. Idols are visible and earthly; God is invisible and heavenly. Idols are powerless; God is all-powerful. He is the Creator of the universe and the Creator of all humanity.

You cannot claim to have turned from idols to the living God if you're still serving the false idols of your selfish ambitions, your greed and lusts, your habits and addictions, your obsessions and unhealthy relationships. Turn to Christ, and he will set you free from slavery to sin so that you can fully and freely serve the living God.

Finally, Paul commends the Thessalonians for waiting expectantly and hopefully for Jesus, whom God raised from the dead—"Jesus, who rescues us from the coming wrath" (verse 10). We live in a time when the church is splintered into a wide variety of movements and denominations. Various teachers, authors, and churches promote an array of "gospels" such as the prosperity gospel, the social gospel, and the post-evangelical "gospel" of the emerging church. But none of these are the true gospel of Jesus Christ, which he commissioned us to preach to every creature on the planet.

There are many "gospels" that make no mention of our fallenness, our sin, our need for a Savior, the blood of Christ, the resurrection of Christ, and the return of Christ. But there is one unmistakable sign of authentic believers: *they are waiting for their Lord's return.*

Paul mentions the Lord's return here in the concluding verse of 1 Thessalonians 1, and he will return to this subject and explore it in detail in later chapters. But here he is simply saying: An authentic follower of Jesus Christ is not panicked over false prophecies about the end times. An authentic follower of Jesus Christ waits and serves and expects Jesus to return at any time. The proof that you are truly waiting for the Lord is that you are sincerely serving him.

We often think of waiting as something we do passively, inactively. We wait in line at the DMV, we wait for a bus, we wait in the doctor's office or the dentist's office. But when the Bible speaks of waiting for the Lord's return, it is not speaking of being inert and passive. Biblical waiting is active and productive. Those who wait for the Lord's return are a blur of activity, and their actions are focused on serving God and others. Those who wait for the Lord are busy witnessing, serving the poor, caring for the sick, feeding the hungry, sheltering the homeless, and comforting the afflicted.

In Luke 19, Jesus tells the story of a nobleman who leaves his servants in charge while he goes on a trip to a far country to receive the kingdom. This nobleman, who represents Jesus, expected his servants to work hard and put his resources to profitable use. There was only one servant the nobleman punished when he returned—the servant who waited passively and achieved no profit. Waiting and serving go hand in hand. If you are truly waiting for your Lord to return, and you want to hear him say, "Well done, good and faithful servant," then make sure that you are actively waiting, actively serving, actively doing God's will as you wait.

These are troubled times—but Jesus the Master is returning soon. He could be here any moment, even before you finish this book. In the coming chapters, we will see what we need to do to be ready for his return.

2

FACING OUR CRITICS

1 Thessalonians 2:1-16

A friend once asked me, "How do you handle criticism?"
"Not very well," I said.
Now, as I mentioned in the previous chapter, how I respond
to criticism really depends on who the critic is. If a nonbeliever criticizes me for declaring that Jesus is the way, the truth, and the life, and
the only way to God the Father, well, I gladly wear such criticism as a
badge of honor. It means I'm being faithful to my calling as a minster
of the gospel.

But if my critic is in the church, if my critic is judging my motives,
if my critic is doubting my sincerity, that's a little harder to take. But I
still have an obligation to respond in a Christlike way. There are sound
biblical principles for dealing with criticism, and we find four of those
principles in the second chapter of 1 Thessalonians. Let's examine each
in turn:

First, we need to expect opposition. We should understand that whenever we boldly proclaim the truth of God's Word, someone will oppose
us. It's inevitable. The world is hostile to God's truth and tries to silence
God's message at every opportunity.

Second, we need to examine the source of the criticism. Who is the
critic? Why is he or she opposed to our message? Has our message
touched a sore spot in the life of the critic?

Third, we need to lower our defenses and ask ourselves, "Is there validity to this criticism? Is there something I could have done better? Is there some lesson I can learn from this criticism?" In this way, we can turn our critics into coaches. We can ask our critic, "How could I have handled this better? What should I do differently next time?" When you ask a critic for insight and help, that critic will probably go from being hostile to being helpful.

Of course, you won't be able to reason with every critic. Some people are negative and judgmental by nature, and you won't be able to change them. The great evangelist Dwight L. Moody had a woman in his congregation who was that kind of critic. She once approached him and said, "Mr. Moody, I don't like the way you do evangelism."

Moody said, "I don't much like the way I do it, either. Tell me, how do you do it?"

The woman stammered, "Um, uh, well, I don't do evangelism."

"Well," Moody said, "I prefer the way I *am* doing it to the way you are *not* doing it."

I have often found that those who can do, *do*. And those who don't do, *criticize*. If you ask your critics how they do what they are criticizing you for, you may learn something—but at the very least, you may silence your critics.

Fourth, don't take criticism personally. That's not easy, especially when the criticism is delivered in a personally condemning or attacking fashion. It can be painful to receive constructive criticism from a friend—yet we know, as the Scriptures remind us, "Faithful are the wounds of a friend" (Proverbs 27:6 KJV). But when our *enemies* criticize us, their intent is rarely constructive. They usually want to hurt us and harm us. It's hard not to bristle at these attacks. The most natural impulse in the world is the urge to retaliate.

But God calls us to move beyond our natural impulses and to seek to respond in a supernatural way. He calls us to love our enemies and to bless those who curse us. In other words, don't take criticism personally. Let it roll off you like water off a duck's back. Let the Lord be your defender.

If you are afraid of criticism, there's a simple way to make sure you are never criticized. The American writer and philosopher Elbert

Hubbard explained it this way: "To avoid criticism, do nothing, say nothing, and be nothing." The problem with this approach is that Jesus has called us to do something, say something, and be something. He calls us to *do* the work of feeding the hungry and comforting the afflicted. He calls us to *speak* that good news to all nations. He calls us to *be* salt and light in a dark and dying world.

So if we are going to be obedient to the Lord, we will need to develop a hide like a rhinoceros when it comes to criticism. Remember, they criticized the Lord Jesus, the perfect, sinless Son of God. If we follow his example, if we stand for his truth, then how can we expect to escape criticism?

WOUNDED BY CRITICISM

The apostle Paul faced critics wherever he went. His critics actually pursued him from town to town to confront and oppose him. His harshest critics were a group of unloving legalists known as the Judaizers. These Judaizers were in the church; they claimed to be Christians. But for them, the gospel of salvation by grace through faith was not enough. They claimed that all Christians, including Gentile Christians, needed to observe the rituals of the Jewish law. They said that all Christian men needed to undergo circumcision, and all Christians needed to keep every point of the Law of Moses.

The Judaizers were vicious opponents of Paul when he was in Thessalonica. Acts 17 tells us that Paul escaped from Thessalonica when the enemies of Christ wanted to kill him. It broke Paul's heart that he could not spend more time with the Thessalonian Christians, teaching them and helping to establish them in the faith. After he was in the city for only three weeks, his enemies ran him out of town.

While Paul was away from Thessalonica, the Judaizers in the Thessalonian church took advantage of Paul's absence. They saw this as an excellent opportunity to undermine his authority and attack the gospel of grace. So they launched a smear campaign. Paul, in the second chapter of this letter, reminded the Thessalonian believers of the opposition he suffered from these troublemakers:

You know, brothers and sisters, that our visit to you was not without results. We had previously suffered and been treated outrageously in Philippi, as you know, but with the help of our God we dared to tell you his gospel in the face of strong opposition. For the appeal we make does not spring from error or impure motives, nor are we trying to trick you. On the contrary, we speak as those approved by God to be entrusted with the gospel. We are not trying to please people but God, who tests our hearts. You know we never used flattery, nor did we put on a mask to cover up greed—God is our witness. We were not looking for praise from people, not from you or anyone else, even though as apostles of Christ we could have asserted our authority. Instead, we were like young children among you.

Just as a nursing mother cares for her children, so we cared for you. Because we loved you so much, we were delighted to share with you not only the gospel of God but our lives as well. Surely you remember, brothers and sisters, our toil and hardship; we worked night and day in order not to be a burden to anyone while we preached the gospel of God to you. You are witnesses, and so is God, of how holy, righteous and blameless we were among you who believed. For you know that we dealt with each of you as a father deals with his own children, encouraging, comforting and urging you to live lives worthy of God, who calls you into his kingdom and glory.

And we also thank God continually because, when you received the word of God, which you heard from us, you accepted it not as a human word, but as it actually is, the word of God, which is indeed at work in you who believe. For you, brothers and sisters, became imitators of God's churches in Judea, which are in Christ Jesus: You suffered from your own people the same things those churches suffered from the Jews who killed the Lord Jesus and the

prophets and also drove us out. They displease God and
are hostile to everyone in their effort to keep us from speaking to the Gentiles so that they may be saved. In this way
they always heap up their sins to the limit. The wrath of God
has come upon them at last (1 Thessalonians 2:1-16).

The Judaizers were miserable people who called themselves Christians, yet they built nothing, accomplished nothing, and never led
anyone to Christ. In fact, they opposed Paul's effort to take the gospel to the Gentiles (that is, the Greeks, Romans, and other non-Jews).
Their mission in life was purely negative, never constructive or positive. Their goal was to stop, stamp out, squelch, and silence those,
like Paul, who were building up the church and spreading the good
news. They infiltrated the Thessalonian church and slandered the
apostle Paul.

How did they oppose Paul? They took advantage of his absence and
twisted the truth to destroy his reputation. They said, in effect, "Paul
said he came here to teach you and to build you up in the faith. Well,
where is he? He ran away, didn't he? He hasn't been seen or heard from
since. He's obviously insincere—one of those fly-by-night preachers,
a charlatan, a fraud. He's only in it for himself. He doesn't really care
about you and what you're going through here in Thessalonica. He has
abandoned you. All he cares about is saving his own skin."

So Paul spends a few paragraphs reminding the Thessalonians of
his ministry among them—how he endured opposition to bring the
gospel to Thessalonica, how he labored among them, not out of selfish or impure motives, not for personal gain, not for praise from people, but out of a sincere love for the Thessalonians. He compares his
love for them to a mother's love for her nursing infant. He compares
his encouragement of them to the way a loving father deals with his
own children. He speaks with compassion and empathy of the suffering and persecution the Thessalonian believers have endured.

Then he addresses the problem of the critics and opponents who
have attacked his reputation. These are the same kinds of people who
killed the prophets in Old Testament times, who plotted and killed the

Lord Jesus, and who drove Paul and his associates out of Thessalonica. They oppose the gospel, they displease God, they are hostile to all that is good, and they are heaping up judgment and wrath for themselves.

It seems that some of the weaker Thessalonians had been swayed by these false Christians and their criticism. After all, the Judaizers knew how to make a plausible-sounding case. They were glib and persuasive. And many of the Thessalonians bought their bill of goods, much to Paul's dismay.

Sometimes in his letters, Paul seems so strong and confident, so full of faith, that he appears to be a spiritual superhero. But Paul was as human as you and I. Cut him and he bleeds. Slander him and he feels the wound. Criticism and opposition always hurt. Yes, we can reach a stage of spiritual maturity where we are better able to manage our pain and forgive an injury, but only a person with ice water in his veins could say that criticism doesn't hurt.

Paul looked to the example of Jesus. He was comforted in knowing that his Lord and Savior, his role model, was constantly criticized and attacked. The Lord's enemies called him a glutton, a drunkard, a lawbreaker, a blasphemer, a seditionist, and a demon-possessed madman. Evil always tries to portray good as evil and evil as good. Evil men always try to create confusion and divert attention from their wickedness.

One way evil people try to confuse the issue is by claiming that those who stand for biblical morality, for God's truth, for the gospel of Jesus Christ, are guilty of that most vile of all sins, the sin of intolerance! If a Christian supports God's model for Christian marriage and the Christian family—one man and one woman raising children in the nurture of the Lord—that Christian will be labeled a bigot and be accused of intolerance. By supporting what is godly and good, a Christian will be demonized as a hater.

It happens again and again, with increasing frequency, in our media, in our social institutions, in our political institutions, and throughout our post-Christian culture. Evil people spread confusion, defining evil as good and good as evil. The issues may change, but the tactics remain the same.

STEWARDS OF THE GOSPEL

When Paul responds to criticism and opposition, he does not give in to anger or self-justification. His response is focused entirely on defending the gospel itself. He reminds the Thessalonians of his love for them. He wants them to know that the gospel he preached to them was delivered in love, not out of any selfish motive. If Paul's motives had been tainted, the gospel he preached might have been tainted as well. Paul wanted the Thessalonians to know that the gospel they received from him was pure and trustworthy.

He did not sugarcoat the message. He did not try to manipulate the Thessalonians or exploit them for his personal profit. He came in a spirit of integrity, without an ounce of hypocrisy, without anything to conceal.

Paul alluded to the outrageous treatment he and his companions received in Philippi. Acts 16 tells how Paul and Silas were preaching in Philippi, and Paul cast a demon out of a slave girl who was used for fortune-telling. When the girl's owners found out that she no longer had a demon and no longer told fortunes, they started a riot. The mob beat Paul and Silas, and the local officials tossed them into jail. There they were kept under filthy conditions in iron stocks.

Despite their beaten and sore bodies and their immobilized limbs, they sang songs and praised God. That night, the Lord sent an earthquake that miraculously threw open the prison doors. The jailer rushed in, brought Paul and Silas out of the prison, washed their wounds, and they were set free. The violence of the mob did not intimidate them. The injustice of false imprisonment did not shake their confidence. The threats of government officials did not deter them from preaching the truth.

The hatred of Paul's enemies made him even more fearless and daring. When you are committed to speaking the truth, your enemies will come after you with clubs and stones—but in the midst of your persecution, whether you live or die, whether you're delivered by an earthquake or martyred by the mob, you'll experience God's power and peace and comfort as you have never experienced it before.

Paul was so consumed with pleasing the Lord that he was never tempted to become a people pleaser. The Lord is the true examiner of motives and thoughts. Paul never worried about what his critics might say. His only thought was, "What does the Lord think of me?" Whenever Paul got up to speak before an audience, he was performing for an audience of One. Only one opinion mattered to Paul, and that was the opinion of his Lord and Savior, Jesus Christ.

In this passage, Paul uses three metaphors to describe his life and ministry among the Thessalonians. First, he said he was a *steward*, not the owner of the gospel he preached. He said that he came as one who was "approved by God to be entrusted with the gospel. We are not trying to please people but God, who tests our hearts." Second, he said he came in a spirit of love and caring, like "a nursing *mother* [who] cares for her children." Third, he said he came in a spirit of instruction, who dealt with them "as a *father* deals with his own children."

Paul saw his ministry as an act of stewardship. He did not work for himself. He was called by God and employed by God to be a good steward of the gospel. This means he felt a steward's obligation to guard the integrity of the gospel with his life. He also felt a steward's obligation to be accountable to the Owner of the gospel, who is the Lord himself. He felt a steward's obligation to follow the Owner's instructions and to work diligently to achieve the Owner's goals and obey the Owner's wishes.

A faithful steward does not allow pride, greed, or the desire to be popular taint his motives. He will not be lured or tempted into disobedience. That's why, Paul explained, his message was true to God's instruction. His motives were pure toward God—and toward the Thessalonians. All of his actions and methods were open and aboveboard.

Why did Paul think it necessary to underscore the obligation he felt as a faithful steward of the gospel? Because stewards are sometimes tempted to go into business for themselves. Many people today are exploiting the gospel for personal gain. They live in big houses and fly in private jets, purchased by people who give sacrificially to their organizations. Paul could have profited from the gospel as well, but he wanted the Thessalonians to know that his motives were pure, and the gospel he preached to them was untainted by greed or the ambition for fame.

You and I are stewards as well. Like Paul, we have been entrusted by

God with the good news of Jesus Christ, and we need to manage this precious asset with absolute integrity and purity. We need to share the good news with everyone around us.

We also need to be good stewards of the time and resources God has entrusted to us. Some people are faithful stewards in giving a tithe—10 percent of their income—to the Lord. But after giving that 10 percent, many Christians feel they can do whatever they want with the rest. Not true. God is as interested in the 90 percent as he is with the 10 percent.

We are stewards of our finances, which God has entrusted to us. We are stewards of our time, which he has entrusted to us. We are stewards of the gospel, which he has entrusted to us. We are stewards of all that we are and all that we have. We own nothing, not even ourselves. We have to give an account to the Master.

LIKE A MOTHER, LIKE A FATHER

Paul described himself as nurturing, like a mother. A faithful mother would never exploit her children, mislead her children, or use her position as their mother for selfish ends. On the contrary, a mother is nurturing, self-sacrificing, gentle, and affectionate. Paul is saying that he and his companions in ministry were faithful not only to share the truth of the gospel but to share their own lives as well. Like a loving mother, Paul unselfishly set aside his needs for the sake of the Thessalonians.

Paul also compared himself to a father—a loving father who instructs and corrects his children. Godly fathers teach their children the life-principles of the Word of God. Children are free to do all sorts of things they enjoy—playing indoors, playing outdoors, running in a field, throwing a ball, riding a bike, and skateboarding. All of these are good, healthy activities, and most fathers encourage their children to play and have fun.

But godly fathers also instruct their children in the Word of God. As God said through Moses:

> These commandments that I give you today are to be on your hearts. Impress them on your children. Talk about

them when you sit at home and when you walk along the road, when you lie down and when you get up. Tie them as symbols on your hands and bind them on your foreheads. Write them on the doorframes of your houses and on your gates (Deuteronomy 6:6-9).

We are to teach our children the principles of God's Word at all times—in the morning, during the day, at night, at every opportunity. We are to keep God's Word before us at all times, bound on our hands and heads, written on the door frames of our homes and on our gates. A Christian father has an obligation before God to strengthen the convictions of his children, to demonstrate Christian courage to them, to train in biblical precepts, and to lead by example.

Godly fathers say to their children, "Watch how I live. See how I walk with God. Observe how I exercise wisdom. See how I testify to others about Christ. Notice that I am not ashamed of the gospel. See how I try to live every day as a man of absolute integrity. And sometimes, as you watch my life, you will see me fail—but watch how I repent and confess my sins and turn back to the Lord for forgiveness and healing."

Now, you might say, "I never had that kind of father. My father was not a godly man. He was not a loving man. He did not instruct me in God's Word. You just don't know my father." It's true. I may not know your father, but God still wants us to follow the example of our Father in heaven. That's the lesson a football player named Dave Simmons learned in the course of his relationship with his earthly father.

Simmons was a defensive back with the St. Louis Cardinals, the New Orleans Saints, and the Dallas Cowboys. His father was a harsh and demanding military man who rarely had a kind word for young David. The father's parenting philosophy was that a child should never be affirmed, but should always be pushed to reach for new goals.

When Dave was just a little boy, his father gave him an unassembled bicycle and told him to put it together. Dave struggled to assemble the bike until he gave up in tears. His father said, "I knew you couldn't do it." Then he assembled the bike himself.

When Dave began playing football in high school, his father criticized him relentlessly. No matter how well Dave played, no matter what he and his team accomplished, his father would come up to him after the game with a list of mistakes he had made or areas where he could improve. Dave's father never had a positive, encouraging, or affirming word for him. "Most boys got butterflies in the stomach before the game," Dave recalled. "I got them afterwards. Facing my father was more stressful than facing any opposing team."

After high school, Dave received scholarship offers from a number of great football schools. He chose to play at the University of Georgia because it was the farthest school from home that offered him a scholarship. He had a successful college career and went into the NFL draft, where he was selected by the St. Louis Cardinals as their second-round pick (Joe Namath, who later signed with the New York Jets, was the Cardinals' first pick).

Dave excitedly called his father to tell him he had been drafted by the Cardinals. Instead of congratulating Dave, his father replied, "How does it feel to be second?"

Those words stung, but Dave Simmons refused to surrender to bitterness toward his father. During his college years, he had received Jesus Christ as his Lord and Savior, and God was prompting Dave to forgive his father and try to build a relationship with him.

In the years that followed, Dave would visit his dad and talk with him, asking him questions about his early years. Dave's father had rarely talked about his own childhood, but as Dave questioned him, his father began to open up. Dave learned that his grandfather had been a tough lumberjack with a nasty temper. Once, his grandfather had taken a sledgehammer to a pickup truck and destroyed it—simply because it wouldn't start. Dave's grandfather had also beaten Dave's father when he was a boy and never had a positive word to say to him.

These conversations opened Dave's eyes to the kind of upbringing his father had experienced. "It helped me see that, under the circumstances, he might've done much worse," Dave recalled. "By the time he died, I can honestly say we were friends."[8]

When Paul uses the metaphor of the loving mother or a loving father, you may or may not identify with that image. That's why it is important for us, as Christian parents, to set a godly example before our children. We model to them what the love of God is like—for better or worse. And if we have grown up struggling with unloving, uncaring parents, perhaps there are reasons why our parents are the way they are. Maybe if we try to understand, we can heal the relationship—and we can forgive.

By using the image of a loving father who instructs his children, Paul is saying it's not enough to merely be compassionate and nurturing like a loving mother. We also need to live exemplary lives and refuse to compromise the truth. Godly fathers love, instruct, and teach their children.

Many churches today do a good job of exemplifying a kind of motherly caring and nurturing toward their parishioners. But many do a poor job of instructing believers in the uncompromised truth of the gospel. Many churches do not offer an image of authentic Christian manhood. There is a lot of grace in those churches, but not much truth. There is a lot of nurturing, but not much instruction.

The church in America today needs to teach the uncompromised truth. The church needs to display courage in the face of opposition and criticism. The church needs to build up the saints in wisdom and integrity, so that they will stand firm for God's Word.

NOT AFRAID TO BE UNPOPULAR

In response to the severe criticism the false teachers leveled at Paul, he reminded the Thessalonians that he lived among them as a steward of God's Word. He nurtured them as a mother. He instructed them as a father. And he communicated the good news among them.

Do you and I fully understand the weight of the precious asset that has been entrusted to our care? Do we understand what it means to be faithful stewards of the gospel?

A faithful doctor feels the burden of being the steward of the life and well-being of his or her patients. A faithful construction engineer feels the burden of being the steward of the structure he is building. A faithful executive feels the burden of being the steward of the organization he leads.

And a faithful steward of the gospel knows that he or she is responsible to clearly announce the good news of Jesus Christ. A good steward will not alter or water down the truth. A good steward will not exploit the truth for personal gain. A good steward will faithfully obey the instructions of the Master.

But there the responsibility of a steward of the gospel stops.

You and I are responsible to proclaim the good news. But the burden for what happens *next* belongs to God alone. It is up to God to see that the gospel message goes out to the people he has elected to save. It is God's responsibility to change hearts. It is God's responsibility to overcome objections. It is God's responsibility to convict people of sin. It is God's responsibility to call sinners to himself for mercy and forgiveness.

Paul faithfully announced the good news. But it was the Word of God that changed hearts. The power of the gospel is not in the messenger but in the message. That power is transmitted not by the human speaker but by the Holy Spirit. When you bear witness to what God has done in your life, when you share the gospel with a friend or neighbor, that person may accept the gospel or reject it.

If that person rejects the gospel you have faithfully shared, don't feel that you have failed. Leave the results with God. The burden is his, not yours. Your only responsibility is to be a faithful steward of the Word.

Sometimes when we share the good news, people will respond with hostility. The gospel often has that effect on people. A.W. Tozer put it this way:

> God's truth has never been popular. Wherever Christianity becomes popular, it is not on its way to die—it has already died. Popular Judaism slew the prophets and crucified Christ. Popular Christianity killed the Reformers, jailed the Quakers and drove John Wesley into the streets. When it comes to religion, the crowds are always wrong. At any time there are a few who see, and the rest are blinded. To stand by the truth of God against the current religious

vogue is always unpopular and may be downright dangerous. The historic church, while she was a hated minority
group, had a moral power that made her terrible to evil
and invincible before her foes. When the Roman masses,
without change of heart, were made Christian by baptism,
Christianity gained popularity and lost her spiritual glow.
From there she went on to adopt the ways of Rome and to
follow her pagan religions. The fish caught the fisherman,
and what started out to be the conversion of Rome became
finally the conversion of the church. From that ignomin-
ious captivity the church has never been fully delivered.[9]

It's tragic that so many preachers today are scrambling after popularity. They are blind to the spiritual and moral decline of our nation.
So they shade the gospel this way or that, they tweak the message to
make it more palatable to the masses, they water down the truth—just
a bit, just enough to make it inoffensive. They spice it up with a little
get-rich-quick theology, and voilà! It's no longer the good news—it's
the prosperity gospel. They keep the Beatitudes and the Golden Rule,
but they quietly remove the cross and the blood. After all, no one wants
to hear all the gory details of the death of Jesus.

But faithful stewards of the gospel are not afraid to be unpopular, are not afraid to be criticized, are not afraid to be denounced and
opposed and imprisoned and put to death for the sake of the Lord Jesus.
Festus, the Roman procurator of Judea, called the apostle Paul mad.
The pope said of Martin Luther that he ought to be in an insane asylum.
The Roman emperor Julian the Apostate called Bishop Athanasius an
"enemy of the gods," "wicked," and "a clever rascal." John Wesley was
beaten and robbed by a street mob and ridiculed in the press because
he preached the gospel of Jesus Christ. William Booth, the founder of
the Salvation Army, was ridiculed and called insane, and the people
who joined his movements were attacked and beaten.

The great English evangelist George Whitefield (1714–1770) is said
to have preached the gospel more than 18,000 times over his career—
and he was no stranger to opposition and criticism. Like the apostle

Paul, he was committed to pleasing God rather than pleasing men. One day, Whitefield received a hateful letter that falsely accused him of wrongdoing. Whitefield made no attempt to defend himself or retaliate against his accuser. Instead, he wrote a brief and cordial reply:

> I thank you heartily for your letter. As for what you and my other enemies say against me, I know worse things about myself than you will ever know.
>
> With love in Christ,
> George Whitefield

No matter what the enemies of the gospel may do to us—whether they criticize us, ridicule us, assault us, imprison us, or kill us—God calls us to be faithful stewards of the gospel. He calls us to be nurturing, to be instructive, to continuously proclaim the kingdom of the Lord Jesus until he returns.

3

VICTORY OVER SATAN

1 Thessalonians 2:17–3:13

A ntonin Scalia was an associate justice of the Supreme Court of the United States from 1986, when he was appointed by President Reagan, until his death in 2016. He was a highly regarded member of the conservative wing of the high court and a devout Catholic. In 2013, he sat for an interview with Jennifer Senior, a writer for *New York* magazine. During the interview, Senior asked Justice Scalia, "You believe in heaven and hell?"

"Oh, of course I do," he said. "Don't you believe in heaven and hell?"

"No."

"Oh, my."

They chatted for a few moments about Scalia's views on the afterlife. Then, as Jennifer Senior was about to change the subject, Scalia added in a loud whisper, "I even believe in the Devil."

"You do?"

"Of course!" Scalia said. "Yeah, he's a real person. Hey, c'mon, that's standard Catholic doctrine! Every Catholic believes that…If you are faithful to Catholic dogma, that is certainly a large part of it."

"Have you seen evidence of the Devil lately?"

"You know," Scalia said, "it is curious. In the Gospels, the Devil is doing all sorts of things. He's making pigs run off cliffs, he's possessing people and whatnot. And that doesn't happen very much anymore."

"No."

"It's because he's smart."

"So what's he doing now?"

"What he's doing now is getting people *not* to believe in him or in God. He's much more successful that way."[10]

C.S. Lewis would agree with Justice Scalia. In 1942, in the introduction to his satirical novel *The Screwtape Letters*, Lewis wrote:

> There are two equal and opposite errors into which our race can fall about the devils. One is to disbelieve in their existence. The other is to believe, and to feel an excessive and unhealthy interest in them. They themselves are equally pleased by both errors and hail a materialist or a magician with the same delight.[11]

Today, these two equal and opposite errors are alive and well in our society—and even in the church. It is hardly surprising that many secularists, atheists, and agnostics scoff at the notion of a literal fallen angel, a demon called Satan. Yet many people who call themselves Christians, especially in mainline denominations, are equally dismissive of Satan's existence.

At the same time, many people, both unbelievers and Christians, have an unhealthy fascination (even an obsession) with the devil. Unbelievers who are focused on Satan and the occult usually want access to demonic powers. Christians who are obsessed with Satan spend too much time worrying about satanic attacks and not enough time meditating on the power of our omnipotent God. Satan is a created and fallen being, and he is no match for the wisdom and might of our Creator.

Satan and his demons are equally pleased to seduce us into either error. They celebrate if we deny their existence—and they celebrate if we imagine that demons are behind every problem we face.

God wants us to have a realistic and balanced view of Satan and his influence. The Bible clearly teaches that Satan and his demons are real, that this present world is a battlefield where unseen, immensely powerful forces wage war against our souls. But—

Satan is not omnipotent. Only God is.

Satan is not omnipresent. Only God is.

Satan is not omniscient. Only God is.

Job 1 teaches that Satan is a person; he actually comes before God and singles out Job, and he argues his case before God. Luke 4 also describes Satan as a person. There Satan finds Jesus in the wilderness, weak from hunger, and he proceeds to debate Jesus, hoping to tempt Jesus into sin.

The Bible also tells us that Satan is constantly scheming against believers. "Put on the full armor of God," Paul warns in Ephesians 6:11, "so that you can take your stand against the devil's schemes." And elsewhere Paul adds that we should live upright lives, continually practicing Christlike forgiveness, "in order that Satan might not outwit us. For we are not unaware of his schemes" (2 Corinthians 2:11; see also 1 Thessalonians 3:5 and 2 Timothy 2:26). In Matthew 4:6, we see that Satan has a thorough knowledge of the Scriptures—and he twists the Scriptures to achieve his own evil ends.

If you have fallen under the spell of the spirit of this age, and you choose to believe that Satan is nothing but a metaphor or a symbol, then I must warn you that you are violating both the spirit and the letter of God's Word. The Scriptures do not portray Satan as anything other than a real and literal spiritual adversary and destroyer. He is invisible yet powerful. He has intelligence, volition, and a will of his own—and his will is to use human beings to thwart the will of God (if that were possible). He is the source of all that is evil in the world.

NEVER UNDERESTIMATE SATAN'S SCHEMES

In the last few verses of 1 Thessalonians 2 and the opening verses of chapter 3, Paul gives us some intriguing insights into the way Satan operates in the world, and how he attacks and opposes God's people:

> But, brothers and sisters, when we were orphaned by being separated from you for a short time (in person, not in thought), out of our intense longing we made every effort to see you. For we wanted to come to you—certainly I, Paul,

did, again and again—but Satan blocked our way. For what is our hope, our joy, or the crown in which we will glory in the presence of our Lord Jesus when he comes? Is it not you? Indeed, you are our glory and joy.

So when we could stand it no longer, we thought it best to be left by ourselves in Athens. We sent Timothy, who is our brother and co-worker in God's service in spreading the gospel of Christ, to strengthen and encourage you in your faith, so that no one would be unsettled by these trials. For you know quite well that we are destined for them. In fact, when we were with you, we kept telling you that we would be persecuted. And it turned out that way, as you well know. For this reason, when I could stand it no longer, I sent to find out about your faith. I was afraid that in some way the tempter had tempted you and that our labors might have been in vain (1 Thessalonians 2:17–3:5).

Paul tells us that, after he was driven out of Thessalonica by would-be assassins, he made plans to return to that city so that he could encourage the Thessalonians and strengthen them in the faith. But Satan repeatedly blocked his plan. Paul does not tell us the exact means Satan used to keep him away from Thessalonica. But Bible scholars have speculated.

Some say that Paul was kept away by threats from the leaders of the synagogue. Others suggest that Paul's "thorn in the flesh," his unnamed physical impediment (which he called a "messenger of Satan" in 2 Corinthians 12:7) might have kept him away. Others suggest that the scandal in the church at Corinth (which was stirred up by Satan) might have kept him too busy to travel to Thessalonica. Still others believe he stayed away out of concern for the safety of the Thessalonian believers. The Thessalonians evidently knew what Paul referred to, and that's why he didn't state it explicitly. In any case, Paul credits deliberate satanic activity for preventing his return to Thessalonica.

A few verses later, Paul again refers to Satan—this time to Satan's role as the tempter of the believers. While Paul ministered in Athens, he sent Timothy to Thessalonica to help encourage and establish the Thessalonians in their faith. Paul was concerned for the Thessalonians believers because he knew they faced intense persecution. He was eager for a report from Timothy because, as Paul wrote, "I was afraid that in some way the tempter had tempted you and that our labors might have been in vain."

So Satan is an adversary. He seeks to thwart us, harm us, discourage us, defeat us, disrupt our plans to do good and to serve God, and tempt us away from the faith.

Here we see, in stark terms, Paul's purpose in writing this letter. He is writing to show believers how to live in light of the imminent return of Christ. Some people are so focused on the end times that they forget to live for Christ in the here and now. They forget to serve Christ and walk in the power of Christ.

The future is important, but not as important as the present. Someone once said that the past is history, the future is a mystery, but the present is a gift to be used in service to God. Satan wants to distract us from the task at hand. He wants us to focus our attention on the past—on past hurts, past failures, past regrets—because he knows that if we are focused on the past, we will be immobilized in the here and now. Or he wants us to focus our attention on the future—on worries and fears that may never come to pass, or on wishful thinking that never accomplishes anything. He knows that if we are living in the future, we're doing nothing in the here and now.

So let's focus on this present moment. Let's be occupied with serving Christ today. We mustn't let Satan tempt us into being paralyzed by the past or immobilized by the future. Let's dwell in the truth of the present.

Victory over Satan is not achieved through willpower. Victory is achieved through truth-power—the power of the Word of God. It is the power and truth of Scripture that exposes Satan and his deceitful schemes. The only solution to the lies of Satan is to expose them to the bright sunlight of God's truth.

Why did Paul give the Thessalonian believers this explanation of his inability to return to them? Why did he say, "For we wanted to come

to you…but Satan blocked our way"? It's because Satan and his servants—those false "Christians" who were spreading lies and accusations about Paul—were using Paul's absence as an opportunity to sow
dissension and division.

Here we have a prime example of how Satan creates havoc within the
church. And Satan uses the same tactics to create havoc between husbands and wives, parents and children, brothers and sisters, members of
extended families, church families, and between races, ethnic groups, and
nations. Satan specializes in creating mischief and misunderstandings.

One of Satan's areas of specialization is creating suspicion, division,
and estrangement by creating an imaginary case in our minds, often
with very little evidence or no evidence at all. One person makes a
comment, and the other person wonders, "What did she *really* mean
by that?" One person forgets to keep a promise or clean up a mess he
made, and the other person concludes, "That just proves he's *deliberately* disrespectful!"

A friend of mine once said, "Don't connect the dots where there
are no dots to be connected." And a wise old saying reminds us, "Don't
read between the lines—that's where the devil writes." Yet most of us
are quite comfortable connecting unconnected dots and reading where
the devil writes and making snap judgments about other people.

In this section of 1 Thessalonians, we see that Satan was working
overtime on both Paul and his Thessalonian friends. Satan was preventing Paul from returning to Thessalonica to minister to his friends
there—and Satan was at work among the Thessalonian believers, sowing seeds of discord and distrust. By undermining Paul, Satan and the
false teachers hoped to undermine Paul and the gospel.

The Bible tells us again and again that Satan is a schemer, and we
should never underestimate his schemes. That's why Paul says, in
2 Corinthians 2:11, "For we are not unaware of his schemes." Satan
is a master strategist, and one of the tactics he employs is infiltration.
Evangelist and Bible teacher Vance Havner put it this way: "Satan is
not fighting churches; he is joining them. He does more harm by sowing tares than by pulling up wheat. He accomplishes more by imitation than by outright opposition."[12]

By comparing Paul's letter to the Thessalonians with Luke's account in Acts 17, we can see even more clearly how Satan opposed the gospel by creating havoc in Thessalonica. After Paul was forced to flee Thessalonica, an angry mob went to the house of a prominent believer named Jason. The mob mistakenly thought that Paul was staying in Jason's house.

When the rioters were unable to locate Paul, they seized Jason and dragged him to the police station. The ringleaders of the mob, who were leaders of the synagogue and the Jewish community, viewed Paul as a troublemaker. His gospel contradicted their legalistic beliefs, and Paul's influence among the people threatened their political power and social standing. The mob continued to riot until the city officials forced Jason to put up his possessions as a bond to guarantee that Paul would not come back again. Paul may have put off returning to Thessalonica out of fear that Jason and the other believers might have had to forfeit their possessions if he returned.

So Paul faced a serious dilemma. He was torn between wanting to be with the Thessalonian believers and wanting to protect those believers from official retaliation. Satan, the father of lies, saw his opportunity, and he spread the notion throughout the Thessalonian church that Paul had abandoned them, that he didn't care about them. The truth, of course, was that Paul loved the Thessalonian Christians so dearly that it broke his heart to be away from them. Being torn from them was like losing a family member. He compared his grief of temporary separation to an experience of being orphaned.

OUR MOTIVATION FOR SERVING JESUS

Why didn't God intervene to halt Satan's scheme? Satan is powerful, but his power and intellect are no match for God's. Yet Satan managed to thwart Paul's plan to return to Thessalonica. Why?

We do not fully understand God's reasons, but we do know that God permits Satan and the rebellious angels to exercise free will, just as he allows human beings to exercise free will. Though God is sovereign over all, he does not prevent the operation of demonic or human free will, even though Satan's choices and our choices lead to sin and suffering. Yet God is able, in his power and wisdom, to turn Satan's evil to serve his own purposes.

Imagine if there were no satanic opposition in the world. Imagine if Paul's plans could proceed without being thwarted by the devil. Imagine a world without any satanic attacks. It would be a utopia, wouldn't it?

Yet we live in a fallen world, and Satan is the evil god of this fallen world. And because Satan opposed and thwarted Paul's plans two thousand years ago, we have Paul's two epistles to the Thessalonians to guide us and encourage us today. God took the evil Satan did toward Paul and turned it into instruction and blessing for our lives today. As a result, God receives glory for turning satanic evil into good.

Paul told the Thessalonians that he longed to see them because they were his "glory and joy." As he tells them in verse 19, "what is our hope, our joy, or the crown in which we will glory in the presence of our Lord Jesus when he comes? Is it not you?" He relates his longing to be with the Thessalonian believers to the joy he will experience when the Lord returns. The Thessalonians believe in Jesus because Paul witnessed to them and shared the gospel with them. When Jesus returns, Paul will present the Thessalonian believers as the fruit of his faithful witness for Christ. They will be the source of his joy and glory in heaven.

I identify with Paul's words. Yes, I am deeply aware of my own failings and stumblings as a Christian. Yes, I humbly confess the many times I have shown unrighteous anger or poor judgment or a stubborn and self-centered willfulness. God knows my shortcomings, and so do those who know me well.

Yet every day, all my waking hours are motivated by the thought that Jesus will return soon—whether "soon" means in the next instant or ten thousand years from now. I want that first moment when I see Jesus face-to-face to be a moment of joy and glory, when I can present many people to the Lord—people with whom I have shared the gospel, people who have responded to the conviction of the Holy Spirit, people who are alongside me in heaven because I was a faithful steward of the good news.

My failings and shortcomings do not occupy the center stage of my life. I can honestly say that, despite my sins, which are many, I truly live to please the Lord, to faithfully obey him, and to share the good news with all who will listen. The Lord's imminent return is my motivation for serving, sacrificing, speaking, writing, living, and breathing.

I don't serve Christ in order to pile up a record of good works. I am not looking forward to saying to Christ, "See what I have done!" No, I am only looking forward to hearing him say to me, "Well done, good and faithful servant." I want to know, when I come into his presence, that the life I have lived has given the Lord pleasure, not disappointment. I want to know that my witness for him has brought glory, not disgrace, to his name.

I don't ever want to compromise his truth—and his imminent return makes his truth all the more urgent. If my message offends some people, it's not because I seek to be offensive. I always want to communicate God's truth with love and grace. But God's truth is offensive to those who are perishing. As Paul wrote in Galatians 5:11, the preaching of the cross is an offense to this dying world, and the uncompromised gospel often provokes a backlash of opposition.

I take no pleasure in being criticized or opposed or attacked—but Jesus takes pleasure in us when we endure persecution for his sake. I look forward to seeing his face and hearing that he was pleased with the way I lived my life. That's my hope. That's my expectation. That's the source of my zeal for Christ.

The Lord has promised that we would receive crowns in heaven. I don't believe these are literal crowns that we will wear on our heads. I believe these are honors we will receive from the Lord for faithful obedience to him.

When I rise up in the morning, when I eat and drink, when I go to work, when I get up to speak, when I write a book, wherever I am, whatever I do, I want to be totally surrendered to the Lord Jesus Christ. If being surrendered to him causes my critics to misunderstand, to be offended, to be angered, that is a small price to pay when compared to all the fruit of my labor for Jesus. That is a small price to pay for the joy and glory of arriving in his presence along with those who have received the gospel message I have shared.

THE FINAL CHAPTERS ARE NOW BEING WRITTEN

In 1 Thessalonians 3, Paul goes on to speak of the sacrifices he has made out of love for these believers. True love always sacrifices. True love always gives itself away. True love never thinks, "What is in this for me?" True love always places the needs of others ahead of the needs of oneself.

Paul tells the Thessalonian believers that he was intensely concerned for their spiritual welfare. He worried that Satan might tempt them away from a pure and sincere faith in Christ. He could not text them or email them. He could receive no news from them. Finally, Paul reached a point where he could not stand the suspense any longer. He couldn't stand not knowing how the Thessalonian believers were progressing spiritually.

So Paul made a costly sacrifice. He sent Timothy—his young assistant, who was practically his own right arm—on a mission to Thessalonica to encourage the believers and to bring back a report on their spiritual status.

At first, you might not think that this is such a great sacrifice on Paul's part. You would have to understand Paul's situation. He was spending many lonely days and nights in a godless city, Athens, the capital of Greek idolatry. The Greek gods, after all, were not mere myths. Like all the gods of pagan religions—from the bloodthirsty Babylonian, Assyrian, and Canaanite gods to the more sophisticated Greco-Roman gods of the classical age—they were manifestations of demonic activity and demonic deception. They were associated with oracles, fortune-telling, sorcery, astrology, demon possession, false doctrine, and spiritual oppression.

So Paul's work in Athens involved not only evangelism but spiritual warfare. It was difficult, troubling work. Acts 17:16 tells us that while Paul was in Athens, "he was greatly distressed to see that the city was full of idols." Paul relied on his young associate Timothy as a partner in ministry, a partner in prayer, and a fellow spiritual warrior. It was an act of sacrifice to send Timothy to Thessalonica. It was undoubtedly oppressive and stressful to wait in that idolatrous city for news from the Thessalonian church.

Yet Paul chose to endure the loneliness of separation from Timothy rather than the suspense and worry over the believers in Thessalonica. Why was Paul worried for the Thessalonian church? He understood Satan's schemes. He knew that Satan would tempt the believers in their time of suffering to fall away from the faith. And he had good cause to be worried, because Satan has used this form of attack again and again down through history.

I have witnessed this form of satanic attack with my own eyes. Believers, when going through a time of intense trial, are tempted by Satan to think—

"God doesn't love me."

"God has abandoned me."

"God is not hearing my prayers."

"God does not care about my sufferings."

When our thoughts go in that direction, our relationship with God can become cold and distant. We don't abandon the faith, but we just go through the motions of being Christians. We no longer see God as a loving Father. Instead, we see him as distant and remote—perhaps even as an abusive parent.

We won't lose our salvation, but we will lose our joy and our confidence in the Lord. We'll lose our trust in his promises. We'll lose the peace of mind that only God can give. We'll lose a sense of warm fellowship with God.

If you are going through a painful time of trial, I want you to know that God loves you. He hears your prayers and he's answering them, even though you may not see the answer right now with your physical eyes. Don't let Satan have this victory over you. Keep trusting God with your eyes of faith.

Next, imagine the thrill and joy Paul felt when Timothy returned with a glowing report on the spiritual state of the Thessalonian believers. Paul writes:

> But Timothy has just now come to us from you and has brought good news about your faith and love. He has told us that you always have pleasant memories of us and that you long to see us, just as we also long to see you. Therefore,

brothers and sisters, in all our distress and persecution we were encouraged about you because of your faith. For now we really live, since you are standing firm in the Lord. How can we thank God enough for you in return for all the joy we have in the presence of our God because of you? Night and day we pray most earnestly that we may see you again and supply what is lacking in your faith.

Now may our God and Father himself and our Lord Jesus clear the way for us to come to you. May the Lord make your love increase and overflow for each other and for everyone else, just as ours does for you. May he strengthen your hearts so that you will be blameless and holy in the presence of our God and Father when our Lord Jesus comes with all his holy ones (1 Thessalonians 3:6-13).

In the midst of all their afflictions, the Thessalonians were standing strong in the Lord. They lived in a culture that was almost completely hostile to the gospel, yet they endured the persecution and peer pressure with a strong faith and a great love for the Lord.

Paul tells the Thessalonians that he has been praying for them night and day—and praying for an opportunity to come encourage them in the faith. Though Paul was separated from the Thessalonians and had no way to communicate with them, he trusted God to hear and answer his prayers.

We don't always see that our prayers are being answered. We may pray for a problem with an unbelieving spouse or a wayward child or a health crisis or a financial struggle that just goes on and on. As we pray, we wonder, "How long? When will God answer my prayer?" And we're tempted to throw in the towel and say, "What's the use? God isn't listening to my prayers."

Don't yield to that temptation. Like the apostle Paul, keep praying, keep asking and seeking and knocking on the door of heaven. God is at work in your life. An answer is coming.

And as you pray, keep this thought before you: The Lord could return at any moment. He could come before you finish reading this sentence. Knowing that Jesus will return with his holy ones to end suffering and establish justice on the earth motivated Paul to keep working, preaching, and praying.

Does the thought of the Lord's return energize you and motivate you to live obediently for him? Does that thought compel you to tell others about Jesus? Does it give you a sense of urgency as you think of your neighbors, your coworkers, your fellow students on campus, the other soldiers in your military unit?

Think of this: Satan knows that the Lord is coming soon—and that thought fills him with terror. He is desperately causing all the trouble and suffering he can right now because he knows his doom is coming. It's only a matter of time before he's bound forever in the lake of fire.

Whatever you're going through, whatever sufferings or setbacks or temptations you are enduring right now, remember that the final chapters of history are already being written. The destroyer will soon be destroyed. Our enemy will soon be defeated. And the Lord Jesus will reign victorious over all.

OUR ENEMY IS MORTALLY WOUNDED

I once heard of an incident that happened to a missionary who lived out in "the bush," the wild region in the northern outback of Australia. He left home for a few days and came back to find a huge python inside his house. He ran to his truck and took out his .45, then he returned to his house and confronted the massive snake.

He took precise aim and fired a single shot into the snake's head. It was a mortal wound—but the python didn't die instantly. Instead, the creature thrashed about with horrible violence. Frightened, the missionary ran from the house and waited outside. He listened to the sound of furniture crashing, lamps shattering, and framed pictures being knocked from the walls.

Finally, the sounds died away. The missionary waited a few minutes longer, then he carefully opened the door and stepped inside. He found the snake dead and still, surrounded by wreckage that had once been his furniture. Debris was everywhere. Wooden chairs were broken in half. Shattered glass littered the floor.

Satan is just like that python. In Genesis 3:15, God foretold Satan's doom when he said to the serpent in Eden,

> "I will put enmity
>   between you and the woman,
>   and between your offspring and hers;
>   he will crush your head,
>   and you will strike his heel."

That prophecy was fulfilled on the cross. There, Jesus shot the serpent in the head. The serpent is mortally wounded—but he's not dead yet. He is still thrashing furiously, still trying to do as much damage as he can, still trying to deceive God's people.

Soon, Satan's thrashing will stop. He will be cast into the lake of fire, and all his evil and hate and rage will be consumed in the flames.

But you and I will be with Jesus in the New Jerusalem. There we will be rewarded for our faithfulness. Jesus is coming soon. That thought makes all the trials of this life worthwhile.

4

LIVING TO PLEASE
THE ONE WE LOVE

1 Thessalonians 4:1-12

In 1993, Jewish-American social critic Dennis Prager penned an important essay for *Crisis Magazine* titled "Judaism's Sexual Revolution: Why Judaism (and then Christianity) Rejected Homosexuality." He opened the piece with a startling statement:

> When Judaism demanded that all sexual activity be channeled into marriage, it changed the world. The Torah's prohibition of non-marital sex quite simply made the creation of Western civilization possible. Societies that did not place boundaries around sexuality were stymied in their development.[13]

Is this true? Did Judaism and Christianity actually create Western civilization by reserving human sexual expression exclusively for marriage? Prager goes on to make a thoroughly researched, soundly reasoned case.

In the ancient non-Jewish world, the uncontrolled sex drive dominated all of life, including religion. All non-Jewish religions worshiped gods and goddesses who engaged in every depraved sexual practice imaginable, including bestiality and rape. The Babylonian goddess Ishtar seduced the warrior Gilgamesh. In the Egyptian religion, the god Osiris committed incest with his sister, Isis, who gave birth to the god Horus. The Hindu god Krishna had many wives, and his son, the god Samba, seduced mortals of both sexes. The Canaanite gods were sexually promiscuous and depraved. Tales from the Greek and Roman pantheons include acts of seduction, abduction, and rape by the gods.

The creation myths of many pagan religions declared the universe to be the result of sexual relations between gods and goddesses. Of all the ancient creation texts, only the Genesis account—"In the beginning God created the heavens and the earth"—declared the universe to be the willful, creative act of a rational, all-wise, all-powerful God. And while pagan cultures viewed the sex act as a power play by the strong against the weak (not only weaker women, but defenseless children), the Hebrew Scriptures placed the sex act within a protective and nurturing zone called marriage. Prager explains:

> Judaism placed controls on sexual activity. It could no longer dominate religion and social life. It was to be sanctified—which in Hebrew means "separated"—from the world and placed in the home, in the bed of husband and wife. Judaism's restricting of sexual behavior was one of the essential elements that enabled society to progress...
>
> The Hebrew Bible...has done more to civilize the world than any other book or idea in history. It is the Hebrew Bible that gave humanity such ideas as a universal, moral, loving God; ethical obligations to this God; the need for history to move forward to moral and spiritual redemption; the belief that history has meaning; and the notion that human freedom and social justice are the divinely desired states for all people. It gave the world the Ten Commandments, ethical monotheism, and the concept of holiness (the goal of raising human beings from the animal-like to the God-like).[14]

Prager says he is often asked what was the greatest revelation he derived from his research into ancient religions. His reply: The Bible has to have been the product of divine revelation. Its teachings are too counterintuitive, too opposed to human nature and to the surrounding cultures to have sprung from the human imagination. The result of that divine inspiration was a collection of moral principles and precepts that enabled the creation of Western civilization.

Today, there are many movements within Western civilization that seek to undo five thousand years of moral and cultural progress. Adultery, fornication, pornography, and homosexuality are being treated as normal or even praised as healthy in our society. Even in the church, there are teachers and leaders who are trying to divorce the church from God's Word, who are trying to normalize sexual lifestyles that the Bible condemns as an "abomination."

The bedrock of Western civilization, Prager says, is the "centrality and purity of family life." And the purity of family life can be maintained only when the two partners in the marriage, the man and the woman, live in obedience to God's Word and maintain their sexual fidelity and purity. Those who would seek to erase the biblical boundaries of sexual morality, those who would make so-called "marriage" between two men or two women the moral equivalent of biblical marriage, don't understand what is at stake.

"At stake," Prager concludes, "is our civilization."[15]

THE ANTI-GOSPEL OF
OUR POST-CHRISTIAN CULTURE

In the previous chapter, we saw how Satan schemes against us in order to silence the good news of Jesus Christ. Satan is a deceiver, whom Jesus calls a murderer, a liar, and the father of lies (see John 8:44). In this chapter, we will expose one of his most dangerous and destructive lies, a satanic deception that has overshadowed our post-Christian world. It is the lie that says biblical morality equals bigotry and intolerance, while the headlong pursuit of sinful pleasure is good and healthy.

This satanic lie has metastasized throughout our society like a moral cancer. It says that people are basically good, so whatever they choose to do, including their most depraved sexual practices, is also good and ought to be tolerated. It says that all selfish gratification is natural and should never be judged or condemned. It says that the sex act, which God has reserved for marriage, is simply a form of recreation. It says that gratifying our sexual lusts is more important than building satisfying relationships. It says there should be no restrictions on sexual expression (most people, even those who believe in total sexual freedom, draw the line at sex with minors, but even that restriction is beginning to collapse in our anything-goes culture).

I call this the anti-gospel. It is the false "good news" of our secularized post-Christian culture. It is the message that is whispered to us, sung to us, shouted to us, and preached to us from our TV screens, movie screens, computer screens, radios, smartphones, newspapers, and magazines. It's even being taught in our schools and tolerated in many churches.

It is the lying "gospel" that tells us that morality isn't important, family isn't important, truth isn't important, faith isn't important, and obedience to God isn't important. What's important are the hormones raging in your bloodstream and the lusts of your imagination, burning to be gratified. This deceitful gospel springs from that hateful inhuman intelligence known as Satan. And it is achieving Satan's purpose. It is destroying souls, destroying lives, destroying families, and silencing churches that once preached Christ.

When we yield to the secular gospel of immorality, when we engage in sexual activity outside of the secured protective boundaries of a monogamous marriage, terrible things happen. We stain the deepest part of our identity. We pollute our bodies, the temple of the Holy Spirit. We bring down guilt upon ourselves, crippling our confidence in God's forgiveness. We destroy the foundation of life's most cherished intimate human relationship. We deny the lordship of Jesus Christ and his authority over our lives.

In his day, the apostle Paul recognized the disastrous consequences of sex outside of marriage. First-century Christians, whether in Corinth or in Thessalonica, came to the Lord from a culture in which sexual perversion was an integral part of their religious lives. Sexual promiscuity and debauchery were a normal and accepted part of their pagan culture.

The tragedy of our own Western culture is that, after two thousand years of Christian influence, our civilization is reverting to the paganism and perversion from whence it came. Greek culture was a cesspool of adultery, fornication, homosexuality, incest, transvestism, pornography, and pedophilia—and it was open, it was accepted, it was applauded. In a culture in which priests and priestesses served as temple prostitutes, perversion was even an approved religious practice.

Imagine those early believers who came to Christ out of a dark, wicked, and immoral culture. Imagine what it must have felt like to come into the sunlight of the love and purity of Christ. For the first time in their lives, they began to see what the Christian life looks like and how the Christian gospel brings healing to marriages, families, and communities. That's why Paul, in the opening verses of 1 Thessalonians 4, writes:

> As for other matters, brothers and sisters, we instructed you how to live in order to please God, as in fact you are living. Now we ask you and urge you in the Lord Jesus to do this more and more. For you know what instructions we gave you by the authority of the Lord Jesus.
>
> It is God's will that you should be sanctified: that you should avoid sexual immorality; that each of you should learn to control your own body in a way that is holy and honorable, not in passionate lust like the pagans, who do not know God; and that in this matter no one should wrong or take advantage of a brother or sister. The Lord will punish all those who commit such sins, as we told you and warned you before. For God did not call us to be impure, but to live a holy life. Therefore, anyone who rejects this instruction does not reject a human being but God, the very God who gives you his Holy Spirit (1 Thessalonians 4:1-8).

Here, Paul makes it clear that when he first preached the gospel in Thessalonica, he did not bring them a message that said, "Come to Jesus—but keep living in immorality." He did not preach, "God cares

only about your soul—what you do with your body is your own business." He did not say, "Jesus died on the cross to make you happy, so
whatever makes you happy is fine with him. As long as you are nice
to people and you go to church, God will wink at your adultery, your
obsession with pornography, your sexual promiscuity, your homosexual lifestyle, and on and on." No, all of those messages are lies straight
from the heart of Satan himself.

Paul preached God's crystal-pure truth to the people in Thessalonica: Live to please God, not to gratify the self. Be sanctified, distinct,
and set apart from the surrounding culture. Avoid sexual immorality.
Practice self-control. Don't take sexual advantage of a brother or sister
in Christ. God will punish those who misuse their sexuality by having
sex outside of marriage.

THE QUESTION WE MUST ANSWER

Today, the church desperately needs parents, Bible teachers, Sunday
school teachers, youth leaders, and mentors who will tell the next generation that God deeply cares how we live our lives and how we express
our sexuality. The secular media blasts Satan's anti-gospel into their
brains daily. We need to pray for our children and grandchildren, talk
to them, and build a protective hedge of truth around them. We need
to help them armor their souls against the attacks of Satan.

Above all, we need to make sure that whenever we share the gospel,
especially with young people, we make it clear that accepting Jesus is
more than simply giving intellectual assent to a creed. Salvation con-
sists not only of receiving Jesus as *Savior*, but receiving Jesus as *Lord*. All
too often the evangelical church has preached a false gospel, a hereti-
cal gospel of easy believism, a gospel that says if you just pray a certain
prayer at some point in your life, then you are free to live your life any
way you please.

While it is true that we are saved by grace through faith, not by
works, it is equally true that we demonstrate the genuineness of our
faith by living a life that is pleasing to God. If we say we have faith but
our way of life does not demonstrate our faith, then is our faith genuine?

That's why Paul commends the Thessalonian believers for turning away from idols when they came to Christ. He told them, "For we know, brothers and sisters loved by God, that he has chosen you, because our gospel came to you not simply with words but also with power, with the Holy Spirit and deep conviction...You turned to God from idols to serve the living and true God, and to wait for his Son from heaven, whom he raised from the dead—Jesus, who rescues us from the coming wrath" (see 1 Thessalonians 1:4-5 and 9-10).

Having said that, Paul now writes to them about what it truly means to turn from idols and live for Christ. He shows them that serving the living God includes serving him with their sexual purity. He lays a foundation for this moral instruction by making clear that our motivation for living sexually pure lives is not a slavish obedience to rules and regulations. No, we are motivated by a deep gratitude to God for his love.

Paul wrote, "We instructed you how to live in order to please God" (4:10). In other words, the big question we must ask ourselves is this: Do I want to live a life that is pleasing to God—or pleasing to self? When we face the temptation to engage in adultery or fornication or pornography or any other sexually impure behavior, we are answering that question by our actions. It's that simple: Please God or please self? God's will or my will? Godliness or sin?

I have heard all the excuses, all the rationalizations. I have heard people explain why they really had no choice:

"I was away from home and lonely and before I knew it, I was in too deep."

"He just kept flirting with me at the office, and he broke down my resistance."

"You don't know what it's like to be a teenager today, surrounded by all these temptations."

"Every fantasy imaginable is just a mouse-click away, and it's so addictive. You can't blame me for giving in to temptation."

Regardless of any excuses, the question still stands: Are you a follower of the Lord Jesus Christ—or a follower of your own lusts?

Paul says, "We instructed you how to live in order to please God" and "you know what instructions we gave you by the authority of the Lord Jesus." In other words, Paul says, "These instructions we gave you on sexual purity are not based on my opinion but on the authority of God's Word. There are no gray areas when it comes to sex and sexuality. On God's own authority, we command you to please the Lord." God's word is uncompromisingly consistent on this issue:

> I made a covenant with my eyes
>   not to look lustfully at a young woman.
>   (Job 31:1)

> But a man who commits adultery has no sense;
>   whoever does so destroys himself.
>   (Proverbs 6:32)

> "But I tell you that anyone who looks at a woman lustfully has already committed adultery with her in his heart" (Matthew 5:28).

> In the same way, count yourselves dead to sin but alive to God in Christ Jesus. Therefore do not let sin reign in your mortal body so that you obey its evil desires. Do not offer any part of yourself to sin as an instrument of wickedness, but rather offer yourselves to God as those who have been brought from death to life; and offer every part of yourself to him as an instrument of righteousness (Romans 6:11-13).

> Flee from sexual immorality. All other sins a person commits are outside the body, but whoever sins sexually, sins against their own body (1 Corinthians 6:18).

> Marriage should be honored by all, and the marriage bed kept pure, for God will judge the adulterer and all the sexually immoral (Hebrews 13:4).

And that is only a small sampling of all that God's Word has to say on the subject of sexual purity. From the Old Testament to the New Testament, the Bible speaks clearly and consistently: Sex is for marriage. Any sex act outside of marriage is sin—and it is self-destructive.

PUTTING UP GUARDRAILS

The best way to avoid sexual sin is by avoiding sin in your thought life. Don't let sinful thoughts linger in your mind. That's what Jesus means when he speaks of looking at a woman lustfully. As long as your thoughts are pure, your actions will be pure. Sinful acts always begin with impure thoughts.

When your thoughts are attacked by Satan, when something you see or hear stirs up feelings of lust, put on your armor. Immediately begin praying and singing praises to God. Tell him you want to please him, not gratify your lusts. Ask him for the power to stand firm against temptation. Take a moment to focus on the question: Do I want to please God or gratify the self? Answer it honestly. It will put the temptation you face in a spiritual perspective.

The apostle Paul puts it this way: "Do you not know that your bodies are members of Christ himself? Shall I then take the members of Christ and unite them with a prostitute? Never!" (1 Corinthians 6:15). How can you claim to love God and be grateful to God when you are taking part of the body of Christ—you—and making the body of Christ participate in a sinful act, an act of adultery or fornication or other sexual sin?

Do you love God? Then why are you living selfishly?

As Paul told the Thessalonians, "It is God's will that you should be sanctified: that you should avoid sexual immorality; that each of you should learn to control your own body in a way that is holy and honorable" (1 Thessalonians 4:3-4). That word *sanctified* means "set apart." It is God's will that we live our lives in a way that is "set apart" from the sin-drenched culture that surrounds us. If we love God, then we want to do his will, not our own.

No one is invulnerable. We all face temptation. That's why we need to put guardrails around our lives so that we can maintain control of our thoughts and our behavior.

There are certain situations that we know in advance can lead us into sin. Just as a recovering alcoholic knows he can never go into a bar and have just one drink, you know the situations that will lead you into sin and self-destruction. It may be a certain form of entertainment that stirs lustful thoughts; you might consider replacing it with a Bible study. Maybe the Internet itself is too much of a temptation; I suggest you either unplug from the World Wide Web or install an app on your phone or computer that reports all your Internet activity to an accountability partner.

Stop making excuses. Start putting up guardrails. That's what Paul means when he says, "Learn to control your own body in a way that is holy and honorable." Paul would not tell a nonbeliever to do that because a nonbeliever does not have the power to control his or her own body. Those who are in the flesh are slaves to sin, slaves to their own lusts.

But you and I have the Holy Spirit of God. The Spirit dwells in us and gives us all the power, all the strength, all the wisdom, all the guidance, and all the resolve we need to flee temptation.

If you're single, please hear me: The Holy Spirit can teach you how to develop deep friendships with both sexes. He can teach you how to sublimate your sexual energy and channel your need for human connection into service for others. He can teach you how to overcome your loneliness by helping others and giving of yourself. He can show you the joy of serving God.

And if you are married, please hear me: Through Christian marriage, the Holy Spirit will teach you how to give yourself to your spouse in a selfless way. He will teach you how to repent of the selfish sexual demands you place on your spouse. He will teach you that marriage is not a contract of legalized lust. He will teach you not to take sexual advantage of your spouse and not to withhold sex as a weapon or punishment against your spouse. He will teach you how to be *intimate* with your spouse in a million ways that have nothing to do with being *sexual.* Please don't confuse sex and intimacy. Though sex can enhance intimacy, true intimacy means being emotionally, spiritually bonded with your spouse.

Paul goes on to warn, "The Lord will punish all those who commit such sins, as we told you and warned you before." Why? Because "God did not call us to be impure, but to live a holy life. Therefore, anyone who rejects this instruction does not reject a human being but

God, the very God who gives you his Holy Spirit" (4:6-8). Paul wants us to know that sexual immorality of any kind will be judged by God because sexual sin leads to broken marriages, shattered families, and wounded children.

Make no mistake: God will chastise a believer who disregards his commands regarding sexual purity because that person spurns God's will, disregards God's purpose, defies God's commands, rejects God's love, and tramples God's grace. We dare not discount the reality of God's righteous judgment against sin.

TRUE FREEDOM

In the next section of this passage, Paul transitions from chastity to charity, from purity to productivity. He writes:

> Now about your love for one another we do not need to write to you, for you yourselves have been taught by God to love each other. And in fact, you do love all of God's family throughout Macedonia. Yet we urge you, brothers and sisters, to do so more and more, and to make it your ambition to lead a quiet life: You should mind your own business and work with your hands, just as we told you, so that your daily life may win the respect of outsiders and so that you will not be dependent on anybody (1 Thessalonians 4:9-12).

Paul commends the Thessalonian believers for demonstrating love and care toward one another in Thessalonica, and for contributing to help their needy brothers and sisters throughout the Macedonian region. He goes on to say that every believer should lead a quiet, orderly, productive life, working at his own trade in order not to be a financial burden on others.

Some Bible scholars have suggested that there were those in Thessalonica who were so consumed with waiting for the return of Jesus that they had given up their jobs, become idle, and were now a burden on their brothers and sisters in the church. Paul is not opposed to charity for the truly needy. In fact, he was instrumental in taking up offerings to help Christians who were out of work or who lacked proper food and shelter.

But Paul had no use for anyone who was able to work but chose not to. Those who are capable of working but choose to live off the charity of others are lazy and selfish. We have a huge problem with this attitude in our culture today.

Working productively, supporting oneself and one's family, is a Christian virtue, and it is motivated by our hope of the Lord's return. Paul tells us that our anticipation of the return of the Lord Jesus ought to make us work hard, serve faithfully, and give generously. And we cannot give generously to people in need if we are not productively supporting ourselves and our family, with a surplus for the church and for charitable giving.

Paul calls us to love one another because our Christian love is a sure sign that we have passed from death to life. Love for our brothers and sisters will keep us from being idle and sponging off them. Love for our brothers and sisters will keep us from becoming busybodies who meddle in other people's lives. Love for our brothers and sisters compels us to serve one another in the body of Christ, the church.

There is a principle in the Word of God that we dare not miss: Our unselfishness, our obedience to God, our abstaining from sin and immorality, all of it must be motivated by a love relationship with God, not by fear or legalistic rules.

Let me illustrate. If someone puts a gun to your head and says, "Give me all your money," I suspect you'll do exactly what the gunman tells you to. But you'll have no love or compassion for the gunman. In fact, you'll resent him for terrifying you and forcing you to give him your money against your will.

But if you see someone suffering and in need and you have a deep love relationship with the Lord Jesus, you'll want to reach out and meet that need. You'll give generously out of gratitude for all that the Lord has given you. You'll say, "Here, take this—and if you need anything else, if there's anything I can do to help you, here's my phone number. Call me anytime, and I'll be here for you in the name of Jesus."

God does not put a gun to your head. God invites you into a love relationship with him. And in the process of living in relationship with him every day, he enables you to grow more and more like Christ every day. That growth in your character is what the Bible calls sanctification. It means being set apart for God's use.

The more intimately we know God, the more we love him and the more we want to please him. In our love-relationship with God, we are like little children with loving parents. Children learn at an early age what pleases—and displeases—their parents. A child who truly loves Mommy and Daddy will naturally do the things that please them.

Our love relationship with God can also be compared to a marriage relationship. Husbands and wives instinctively know how to please one another. If the love relationship is strong, if the caring is deep, they will continually do those things that make each other happy—and they will abstain from any actions that would grieve or offend the other.

This same kind of love should motivate our service to God. The Holy Spirit wants to empower us and fill us with that kind of love for him. True freedom is not the freedom to sin but the freedom to serve God and live godly lives out of hearts full of gratitude and love. True freedom is to be free of the tyranny of our fallen selves—our rebelliousness and lusts. True freedom is to be free from enslavement to Satan and sin.

Twice in this passage, Paul uses the phrase "more and more." First, he commends the Thessalonians for living to please God, and he urges them to do so "more and more." Second, he commends the Thessalonians for loving one another, and he urges them to do so "more and more." In other words, with each passing day, we should live to please God and live to serve others more than the day before. Our love for God should grow daily, and so should our love for one another.

Are you growing in your love for the Lord Jesus and your love for your brothers and sisters in Christ? Can you chart your progress from the day you first fell in love with the Lord until today? Is your love growing? What is the evidence that you love him more and more? What is the evidence that you love your fellow Christians more and more?

As you look back over your Christian life, can you point to specific situations, specific actions, specific things you've done and said that prove that you love God and love others more today than yesterday, more this week than last week, more this month than last month, more this year than last year?

Or is your service to God and others regressing and moving backward?

The best-known, worst-kept secret of the Christian life is this: No one can stand still in the Christian walk. If you're not moving forward, you're moving backward. You can't stand still, so keep moving forward with Christ. Keep growing in your love for him, your faithfulness to him, your gratefulness to him, your obedience to him.

When your love for Jesus is real and deep, living to please him is never a burden.

5

GODLY GRIEF AND HEAVENLY HOPE

1 Thessalonians 4:13-18

There's a comment I hear again and again following funerals at our church. It usually comes from a nonbeliever or from someone who is not strong in the faith. The comment is this: "I've never been to a funeral like this before."

I have heard those words hundreds of times. And I know exactly what those people are responding to, even though they may not be able to put their finger on what makes a funeral at our church different. What do they find at our church that they don't find in other funerals they've attended?

Hope.

When a believer dies, and our church family gathers to remember and celebrate that person's life, we always deliver a message of hope. A funeral for a believer who died in the Lord is always an occasion for hope. Whether the funeral is held in our church or another church that believes in the resurrection, that funeral will be an uplifting time of worship and hope.

Why? The reason for our hope is right here in Paul's first letter to the believers in Thessalonica:

> Brothers and sisters, we do not want you to be uninformed
> about those who sleep in death, so that you do not grieve

like the rest of mankind, who have no hope. For we believe
that Jesus died and rose again, and so we believe that God
will bring with Jesus those who have fallen asleep in him
(1 Thessalonians 4:13-14).

Paul begins, "we do not want you to be uninformed about those who sleep in death." When we lack information, our imagination tends to fill in the gaps with the worst possible scenarios. Death is a frightening and mysterious subject to begin with. Ignorance only increases our confusion and fear. Knowledge brings blessing. So Paul wants the Thessalonians—and us—to have reliable knowledge about what happens to believers when they die.

The apostle makes it clear that there is nothing wrong with the emotion of grief. Nowhere does the Bible say that believers should not grieve. Nowhere does the Bible say that we should not shed tears over the loss of a loved one. Nowhere does the Bible say that we do not feel sorrow and a sense of emptiness when a loved one passes away.

But we do not grieve like those who have no hope.

When a nonbeliever dies, his or her loved ones have nothing left but memories. But when a believing loved one dies, we have hope for the future because we believe in the resurrection and in everlasting life. The grief and sorrow we feel is temporary. We are saying, "Goodbye— until we meet again." We are not saying, "Goodbye forever."

So we grieve, because even a temporary separation is painful. We miss our children when they go off to college. We miss our parents when they retire and move to another state. It's only natural that we should miss our believing loved ones when they are promoted to eternal life in heaven. We know we will see them again, but in the meantime, we grieve.

In his letter to the Thessalonians, Paul shows sympathy and understanding for the bereavement we all feel over the loss of a loved one. He does not rebuke them for their sadness or shock. He does not minimize their loss and pain.

The time of loss is a time of looking back on the past, looking forward to the future reunion in heaven, and looking inward and reminding ourselves of our own mortality. When we stand at the grave-side of someone who has died, our false sense of security, our false assumption that life will always go on and never stop, falls away. We are faced with the reality of death—and we should remember that there is a grave waiting for us as well.

But we need not be morbid about it. The grave is not the end of the story. We believe in the empty tomb of the Lord Jesus Christ, and we have absolute confidence that our bodies will one day be raised like his.

Notice that Paul speaks of "those who sleep in death." Sleep is an excellent metaphor for death. When we are asleep, we are temporarily separated from the waking world. We cannot talk to our loved ones while we are asleep. We cannot have fellowship with them while we are asleep. Sleep is a departure from the troubles of this life into a realm of restfulness and peace.

Yet sleeping is followed by waking, just as (for the believer) death is followed by resurrection. There are some who teach that when the believer dies, the soul goes into a deep sleep until the time of the resurrection—but this notion is contrary to what the Bible teaches about death.

Paul tells us that to be absent from the body is to be home with the Lord (see 2 Corinthians 5:8; Philippians 1:23). In Luke 23:43, as Jesus was being crucified between two thieves, he told the repentant thief, "Truly I tell you, today you will be with me in paradise." He didn't promise this dying man that he would be raised again at some unspecified future date—he explicitly said, "*Today* you will be with me."

In Matthew 17:3, Moses and Elijah—two long-dead Old Testament saints—appeared with Jesus on the Mount of Transfiguration. If their souls were sleeping until the day of resurrection, how could they have appeared in a recognizable bodily form?

In Revelation 6, a scene takes place before the resurrection of the saints (we know this because John tells us that, at that time, believers are still being martyred upon the earth). He writes:

> When he opened the fifth seal, I saw under the altar the souls of those who had been slain because of the word of

God and the testimony they had maintained. They called out in a loud voice, "How long, Sovereign Lord, holy and true, until you judge the inhabitants of the earth and avenge our blood?" Then each of them was given a white robe, and they were told to wait a little longer, until the full number of their fellow servants, their brothers and sisters, were killed just as they had been (Revelation 6:9-11).

These martyred believers, who had been slain because of the Word of God, were not sleeping. They were awake and aware and they were calling out to God for justice.

In Luke 16, Jesus tells the parable of the rich man and Lazarus. And it is clear in the story that when a believer dies, he goes immediately into the presence of God—and when an unbeliever dies, he goes immediately into a realm of conscious suffering. That is what Paul means when he speaks of those who die without hope. Their end is terrifyingly hopeless because they are in a place of suffering from which there is no escape. Those who belong to Christ, however, experience the most blessed hope of all: a glorious reward and an eternity of unending joy in the presence of the Lord.

As believers, we don't ever need to apologize for shedding tears at the graveside of a loved one. But our tears are hallowed tears, hopeful tears, confident tears, because we look forward with absolute certainty to the day of resurrection.

CONFIDENCE IN THE LORD AND THE RESURRECTION

Joseph Flacks was an Orthodox Jew who was born in Latvia and emigrated to the United States when he was fifteen. He and his family had survived the "Easter pogroms," when mobs of people who claimed to be Christians persecuted and killed many Eastern European Jews. His family settled in New York City, where he peddled small wares on the streets. As he lived and worked on the sidewalks of that huge metropolis, he looked at the towering steeples of the churches—and he felt a deep bitterness in his heart against all who called themselves Christians.

He grew older and opened his own business, and a number of the employees he hired were Christians. In 1908, one of his employees invited him to attend a revival meeting conducted by British evangelist Rodney "Gypsy" Smith. Joseph Flacks agreed to go to the meeting just to listen to the singing. But the gospel message reached deep into his soul. The next day, Joseph talked to his employee about what he had heard that night—and the employee urged him to talk to his pastor, Harris H. Gregg.

So Joseph Flacks met with Dr. Gregg in the pastor's study. In fact, their meeting stretched out for six hours. They spent almost the entire time talking about the Hebrew Scriptures, which Christians call the Old Testament. Dr. Gregg went through one prophetic passage after another, answering every question Mr. Flacks raised. Finally, Mr. Flacks said, "Doctor, it is enough. I see that, according to my own Holy Scriptures, Jesus is my Messiah. I accept him now as my Savior."

The two men knelt together in prayer, and Joseph Flacks went home and spent the entire night on his knees in prayer.

The next morning, Joseph told his wife and family about the decision he had made for Christ. They thought he had lost his mind. They wept and mourned because this devoutly Orthodox Jewish husband and father had joined the Christians—and weren't Christians the very people who had persecuted him in the old country?

Joseph Flacks was very open and vocal about his newfound faith. Word of his conversion spread throughout the business community. His Jewish employees quit and his Jewish customers deserted him. Within weeks, his business was ruined. His wife left him, his family members shunned him, and his old friends avoided him.

Yet he was not without friends. His Christian friends continued to talk to him, pray with him, and help him financially. Joseph Flacks sensed that God was calling him into full-time Christian ministry. With nothing but two business suits and a few dollars to his name, he went to Chicago and studied at the Moody Bible Institute. He paid for his education by doing manual labor. After three years, he graduated and was accepted as a pastor of a church in Texas.

His ministry flourished, and soon he was speaking at Bible

conferences, sharing his amazing testimony while teaching the Word of God. For almost thirty years, he traveled throughout the United States and Canada, and became one of the most effective soul-winning evangelists in the country. He even traveled to Asia, Palestine, and Europe, and eventually preached the gospel in his homeland, Latvia.

Joseph Flacks lived simply, giving as much money as he could to missions or to a fund to help young people who were preparing for full-time Christian ministry. In time, his health began to fail. On August 14, 1940, he passed out of this life and into the presence of his Lord and Savior, Jesus Christ.

But before he died, Mr. Flacks had cards printed up with a special message for all the people he left behind. He arranged for those cards to be mailed out on the day of his death. The message on the cards read:

TRIUMPHANT THROUGH GRACE

This is to announce: I moved out of the old mud house (2 Corinthians 5:1).

Arrived in the Glory-land instantly, in the care of the Angelic escort (Luke 16:22).

Absent from the body, AT HOME with the Lord (2 Corinthians 5:6).

I find as foretold (Psalm 16:11), In His presence FULLNESS of JOY—PLEASURES forevermore!

Will look for YOU on THE WAY UP at the redemption of the body (Romans 8:23).

Till then, LOOK UP!

J.S. (Uncle Joe) FLACKS[16]

That message was written by a man who had absolute confidence in his Lord and Savior—and in the resurrection to come. He knew exactly where he was going when he died and what he would experience there, and he devoted his life to pointing others to heaven as well.

So let's look at the rest of Paul's message to the Thessalonians regarding the promise of the second coming, the resurrection of the dead, and eternal life in heaven with Christ. The Thessalonian Christians were troubled and confused over the issue of the Lord's return to take his followers to heaven. Their confusion created a deep anxiety about their eternal destiny and the destiny of their loved ones who had already died.

They wondered: What happens to our loved ones when they die? Where are they now? Will I see them again? In the closing verses of 1 Thessalonians 4, Paul addresses their concerns and questions about the second coming of Christ.

THE DEAD IN CHRIST

Apparently, many of the Thessalonian believers were panicked by rumors that the Lord had already returned—that the *Parousia* had taken place and they had been left behind. Paul doesn't want them to be fearful and misinformed, so he addresses their fears and concerns:

> According to the Lord's word, we tell you that we who are still alive, who are left until the coming of the Lord, will certainly not precede those who have fallen asleep. For the Lord himself will come down from heaven, with a loud command, with the voice of the archangel and with the trumpet call of God, and the dead in Christ will rise first. After that, we who are still alive and are left will be caught up together with them in the clouds to meet the Lord in the air. And so we will be with the Lord forever. Therefore encourage one another with these words (1 Thessalonians 4:15-18).

The *Parousia* is popularly known by several names, such as the second coming or the rapture. What will this event look like? Paul explains that the Lord himself will come with a loud command, with the shout of an archangel, and with the trumpet call of God. At that moment, there will be a resurrection—the dead in Christ shall rise first. Then we who are still alive will be caught up to meet the Lord in the air.

The order of these events is important. The Thessalonian believers were afraid that those who had already died were at a disadvantage. But no, those who have preceded us in death are already with the Lord right now. They are like the repentant thief on the cross, to whom Jesus said, "Truly I tell you, today you will be with me in paradise." When they died in Christ, they passed from this life into the presence of their Lord.

When Jesus returns, the dead in Christ will be with him. But, you may ask, doesn't Paul say, "The dead in Christ will rise first"? Doesn't that mean that dead believers are sleeping in the ground, not in heaven with Jesus?

No. When a believer dies, the *body*—not the believer—goes into the ground. As the Scriptures consistently teach, the believer who is absent from the body is home with the Lord. When the Lord returns, he will bring the believers with him. They will not be filmy, ghostlike spirits. They will not be naked souls. They will be clothed in their incorruptible resurrection bodies.

To us, who have not seen our loved ones since we said goodbye to them at their graves, it will seem that they are being resurrected, raised up from the grave. But they have been with the Lord all along, and they will return with him at the second coming, clothed in the same kind of resurrection body as the Lord's own glorified body.

Some Christians say that the dead should always be buried, never cremated, because a body cannot be resurrected if it has been reduced to ashes. According to the Scriptures, that is nonsense. If you die in Christ, you'll receive a new resurrection body, period.

Once you've died, you're finished with your old mortal body. You don't need it anymore, and neither does God. It doesn't matter if your body is buried or cremated or you were eaten by a shark—every believer gets a new and glorified resurrection body. And that is true of every believer who is still alive when Jesus returns. You have God's Word on it.

Remember that at the beginning of this passage, Paul said, "We do not want you to be uninformed about those who sleep in death." Understand, it's the corruptible body that sleeps in death—not the believer. The believer is with the Lord, and all the believers who died in Christ will return with the Lord when he comes to take his church home with him.

So don't feel sorry for the dead in Christ. If anything, they should feel sorry for us! Their worries and sufferings are over—they are enjoying fellowship with the Lord right now. And they will be with him when he returns for that great rendezvous in the sky.

My friend, our sure hope of the return of Christ is not based on the shifting sands of philosophical speculation. It is not built on the shaky framework of ancient mythology. It is not a fable designed to make people feel better about their own mortality. No, the truth of the Lord's return is based upon three well-attested historical evidences:

1. The death of Christ

2. The resurrection of Christ

3. The revelation of Christ

If we believe that Jesus died for our sins and rose again, then by virtue of his substitutionary death on our behalf, by virtue of his payment in full for the wages of our sins, by virtue of his redemptive work on the cross, *we have been saved*. We have been forgiven and accepted by the Father and we will be welcomed into his presence at the moment we pass through the doorway of death.

THE MOST EXCITING NEWS IN THE WORLD

It's important to notice that when Paul refers to the believer's death, he calls it "sleep." But when he refers to the death of Christ, he doesn't resort to metaphors. He calls death what it is—*death*. Why?

Paul is drawing a distinction between the death we die and the death that Jesus experienced on the cross. Our Lord experienced the full fury of death in all its dimensions so that we would have to experience death only as sleep. Jesus experienced the punishment for our sins, so that we might be fully alive to righteousness. Jesus experienced the horrors of death so that death for us would be a peaceful rest.

Then Jesus rose from the dead so that we might be assured of our own resurrection. He triumphed over the grave so that we might catch a glimpse of our own future triumph.

So whether you reach the end of your life and fall asleep in the arms of Jesus, or you are alive and waiting on the day of his return, it makes no difference. On that day, the dead in Christ, the living in Christ, and the Lord himself will all be together on that great reunion day. We will be united at last, never to be separated again. Here is how Paul described that day in his first letter to the believers in Corinth:

> Listen, I tell you a mystery: We will not all sleep, but we will all be changed—in a flash, in the twinkling of an eye, at the last trumpet. For the trumpet will sound, the dead will be raised imperishable, and we will be changed. For the perishable must clothe itself with the imperishable, and the mortal with immortality. When the perishable has been clothed with the imperishable, and the mortal with immortality, then the saying that is written will come true: "Death has been swallowed up in victory."
>
> "Where, O death, is your victory?
>
> Where, O death, is your sting?" (1 Corinthians 15:51-55).

That's the most exciting news the world will ever hear! When I read those words, I feel like bouncing on my heels to get a jump on meeting the Lord in the air.

And just think of this: The Lord *himself* is coming for us. He won't send an angel or an ambassador or a prophet. He loves us so much that he is coming himself. As the angel told the disciples after the resurrected Lord ascended into heaven, "This same Jesus, who has been taken from you into heaven, will come back in the same way you have seen him go into heaven" (Acts 1:11).

But that is not all that is amazing and wonderful about the Lord's return. Paul tells the Thessalonians that the return of Jesus will be accompanied by "a loud command, with the voice of the archangel and with the trumpet call of God" (4:16). Notice the military tone of this statement. The Lord's return will be accompanied by a shouted command, like a general calling to his troops. It is a call to arms. Every one of the Lord's faithful soldiers will hear it. Every one of his soldiers will respond to it. Every one of his soldiers will rejoice in it.

Along with the voice of the archangel, the trumpet will sound—and it will be heard throughout the world. Wherever the Lord's faithful followers are—Africa, Europe, Asia, Australia, the Pacific Islands, the Americas—they will hear the shout of the archangel and the blare of the trumpet. Trumpets have great symbolic importance throughout the Bible. Trumpets have been used to assemble the people. Trumpets have sounded to announce a religious feast. Trumpets have sounded to announce celebrations. Trumpets have heralded great events.

When the Lord returns, the sound of the trumpet will make it clear that the time has come to say goodbye to this fallen world, to say goodbye to temptations and grief, to say goodbye to anxiety and worry, to say goodbye to fear and terror, to say goodbye to tears and sorrow, to say goodbye and good riddance to Satan's attacks and the ravages of sin.

One devout Christian who eagerly looked forward to hearing that trumpet was hymn writer Fanny Crosby. She was born in 1820 and went home to be with the Lord at age ninety-four. During her life, she composed more than eight thousand hymns.

When Fanny was just six weeks old, she developed an inflammation of the eyes, which doctors treated with mustard poultices. The treatment left her blind for life. Because of her blindness, she developed an amazing approach to composing poetry and song lyrics. She always began with a prayer for inspiration, then she would begin composing in her mind, remembering every line of the composition as she went. She would often store up a dozen or more complete hymns in her memory before dictating them to a secretary.

One of her best-loved hymns is "To God Be the Glory." It contains this beautiful description of the believer's hope of the Lord's return:

> Great things He hath taught us, great things He hath done,
>   And great our rejoicing thro' Jesus, the Son;
> But purer, and higher, and greater will be
>   Our wonder, our transport, when Jesus we see.[17]

Fanny Crosby spent almost her entire life wrapped in darkness, unable to see. But she looked forward to the wonder and rapture of seeing Jesus with new resurrection eyes.

THE ULTIMATE REUNION

You've undoubtedly heard people refer to the second coming of Christ as the rapture, but you may not know why. This use of the word derives from the Latin Vulgate translation of 1 Thessalonians 4:17, where Paul writes, "we who are still alive and are left will be *caught up* together with them in the clouds to meet the Lord in the air." The phrase "caught up" is rendered *rapiemur* in Latin, a word that means "caught up" or "carried off." Rapture, then, is an English transliteration of *rapiemur*.

The moment of the rapture will be an unbelievably happy reunion between the living and the dead—and the dead, those who died in Christ, are truly more alive in the presence of Christ than we are here on earth.

This event will be far more important than most of us realize. The day of the rapture will be a day of cosmic triumph—one of the most important days in the history of the universe. On that day, Paul says, we will "meet the Lord in the air." Why is this significant? Because, in Ephesians 2:2, Paul refers to Satan as "the ruler of the kingdom of the air." When we are caught up in the air to meet Jesus, we will literally invade the domain of Satan. The devil's kingdom will fall, and we will take possession of the kingdom of the air in the name of King Jesus.

The kingdoms of this earth will become the kingdom of our God. And we will be with him forever. That will be the ultimate reunion— the reunion of all reunions.

Paul concludes, verse 18, "Therefore encourage one another with these words." The hope of our resurrection and victory over Satan is a message of intense encouragement. No matter what struggles we are going through today, all our problems will be swallowed up by that day of triumph over Satan.

So I ask you: If the rapture were to take place today, can you say with absolute assurance that you would be among those who will be caught up in the air to be with Jesus and his saints? Or would you be among those who will be left behind for judgment?

Only those who live for Christ in the here and now will be united with Christ on that day. Make sure that you are walking with him today so that you can be united with him forever.

6

LIKE A THIEF IN THE NIGHT

1 Thessalonians 5:1-11

I was hired for my first real job in 1970. I worked in the telephone exchange in North Sydney, Australia, just across from the Harbour Bridge. The telephone exchange was next door to a courthouse. Most of the people I worked with went to the pub on their lunch hour, but one other man and I had lunch in the company cafeteria.

One day, my friend suggested that we take our sandwiches and go next door to the courthouse and watch a trial. It seemed like a great way to spend the lunch hour, so we went.

As we sat in the gallery, we could see the solicitors with their robes and wigs, the crown solicitor (or prosecutor), the policemen, and the prisoners. We waited a few minutes, then a door opened and the judge entered the courtroom. The moment he made his appearance, a hush came over the courtroom. The entire atmosphere changed. A solemn mood settled over everyone.

My friend and I sat quietly eating our lunches and watching the proceedings. We had no worries, no anxiety, no apprehension whatsoever about being in that courthouse. We could look the judge right in the eye, boldly and without concern because our names were not on the docket. We were not in the prisoner's seat. No accusations had been lodged against us. We had come as interested spectators, not defendants.

When my friend had suggested we go and watch a trial at the

courthouse, I had thought it would be an interesting experience—and it was. But it was more than that. Watching that trial left an indelible impression on me. I realized how awful it must feel to be a criminal defendant and to know that the people in that room—the lawyers, the jurors, and the judge—would decide my fate. They would decide what is true and what is false. And they would decide whether I was guilty or not guilty.

And if I was found guilty, the judge would impose a sentence.

That experience made me think of how it is going to be for both believers and unbelievers on the day of judgment. Those who place their trust in Jesus Christ will have no fear on that day. They will be like my friend and me, sitting in the gallery, watching the proceedings. They will be fully assured that any judgment against them has been paid in full on the cross of Calvary.

As Christians, we have been declared forgiven—not guilty!—by the Judge himself. He took our punishment and signed our pardon. He raised us out of darkness to the light. He raised us out of death to eternal life. He spared us from punishment and granted us great rewards.

So we, as believers, do not fear the day of the Lord. The only ones who ought to fear the day of judgment are those who reject Jesus, those who think they are good enough to earn a place in heaven by their own efforts, those who think they can be saved by good deeds and charitable work, those who think they have no need of a Savior.

They should fear, they should tremble—and they should place their trust in Jesus before it's too late. That is Paul's message to the church in Thessalonica in the next section of his letter.

A DAY OF TERROR AND REGRET

The believers in Thessalonica were concerned about the return of Christ, the end of the world, the day of judgment, and God's timetable for all these events. In other words, those Thessalonian believers two thousand years ago were not unlike Christians today. So at the beginning of 1 Thessalonians 5, Paul writes:

> Now, brothers and sisters, about times and dates we do not
> need to write to you, for you know very well that the day of
> the Lord will come like a thief in the night. While people are
> saying, "Peace and safety," destruction will come on them
> suddenly, as labor pains on a pregnant woman, and they
> will not escape (1 Thessalonians 5:1-3).

Paul begins with a segue: "Now, brothers and sisters, about times and dates…" As the Thessalonian congregation listened to these words, I'm sure every believer leaned closer, not wanting to miss a syllable that Paul had to say about future events. And I'm sure that many were disappointed to hear the rest of that sentence: "we do not need to write to you, for you know very well that the day of the Lord will come like a thief in the night."

Anyone who was obsessed with knowing the times and dates had the wrong focus. It's not for us to know God's timetable. If God announced in his Word that the date would be centuries in the future, then generations of Christians would be spiritually indifferent and callous and have no sense of urgency about serving the Lord. And if God announced a date that was mere days or weeks away, people would say, "What's the use of going to work and living my life? I'll just go up on a mountaintop and wait for Jesus to return."

God understands that we are clock-watchers by nature. He knows that announcing a date for the return of Christ would only undermine our motivation for serving him. So he keeps his prophetic timetable a mystery to us so that we will live daily in a state of readiness and preparation. If the Lord returns today, wonderful—we'll keep serving until he gets here. If he returns years from now, that's good too—it will give us more time to share the gospel and invite more people into his kingdom.

The Thessalonian believers had probably been told about the Lord's own statement: "But about that day or hour no one knows, not even the angels in heaven, nor the Son, but only the Father" (Matthew 24:36). Despite clear warnings in Scripture, people have been making predictions about the Lord's return for twenty centuries. These

Thessalonian believers had received erroneous information about the end of the world from false teachers who had infiltrated the church, and they were unsettled by it.

So Paul wrote to assure them that they had not missed the Lord's return, that those who had died in the Lord were safe in his presence, and that whenever the rapture would take place, all believers would be changed, would receive their resurrection bodies, and would be instantly taken to heaven to be with the Lord forever. Now, Paul tells them what will happen to the unbelievers—to those who are left behind when Jesus comes.

Paul's warning that the return of the Lord would come "like a thief in the night" undoubtedly touched a nerve with those believers. In the Middle East in the first century, it was not uncommon for burglars to come into a home in the middle of the night. In those days, a house could not be secured as well as today. There were no deadbolt locks, no burglar alarms, and no 911 to call. The man of the house slept lightly and had to defend his own home and family if he heard someone rummaging through his house in the middle of the night.

Robbers did not send out a postcard to say, "On such-and-such a night, I'll be paying you a visit. Please have your valuables gathered together so that I can grab them quickly and be on my way." Thieves always came silently and unannounced—and their goal was to take what they came for and be gone before you ever know they were there.

Paul also uses the metaphor of labor pains to describe the Lord's return. There's quite a bit of difference between a thief coming in the middle of the night and a woman in labor, about to give birth. The thief is totally unexpected. The labor pains, while they may come on suddenly, are certainly not unexpected. The mother has had months to prepare for this event.

For nonbelievers—for all those who have rejected Christ—the day of the Lord is going to come like a thief in the night, without warning, totally unexpected. But for followers of Christ, it's going to be like a pregnancy that culminates in labor pains and the moment of birth. Labor pains are expected and inevitable. We don't know exactly when they will begin, but we are waiting for them and we know they are coming. That's why a pregnant mother is described as "expecting."

Moreover, labor pains, while painful to experience, announce a joyful deliverance. The thief in the night brings calamity and disaster. Labor pains bring rejoicing and new life.

When the day of the Lord comes upon you, I pray that it will come like labor pains—not like a thief in the night. Always be ready. Always be prepared. Always be serving. Always be working. Always be giving. Don't let that day take you by surprise.

The thought of the day of the Lord should not alarm or frighten you. It is not a day to be feared—unless it catches you spiritually unprepared. If you rely on your own good works and good intentions to get you to heaven, if you have placed your trust in yourself instead of in the Lord Jesus, then you have rejected God's only way of salvation. For those who trust in anyone other than Jesus, the day of the Lord will be a day of terror and regret.

FROM DARKNESS TO LIGHT

Next, Paul carries this metaphor further, writing about the importance of being prepared for the coming of that day:

> But you, brothers and sisters, are not in darkness so that this day should surprise you like a thief. You are all children of the light and children of the day. We do not belong to the night or to the darkness. So then, let us not be like others, who are asleep, but let us be awake and sober. For those who sleep, sleep at night, and those who get drunk, get drunk at night. But since we belong to the day, let us be sober, putting on faith and love as a breastplate, and the hope of salvation as a helmet. For God did not appoint us to suffer wrath but to receive salvation through our Lord Jesus Christ. He died for us so that, whether we are awake or asleep, we may live together with him. Therefore encourage one another and build each other up, just as in fact you are doing (1 Thessalonians 5:4-11).

Paul tells us that those who are not expecting the Lord's return are living in spiritual darkness. They are like people who sleep the night away or party the night away in drunkenness, out of their right minds, unprepared for what is about to overtake them. By contrast, Paul says, we as believers do not belong to the night, we are not left in darkness, we are not drunk or asleep. We are awake and sober, ready for the Lord's return.

These are powerful metaphors to describe the state of the unsaved, unprepared soul: Darkness. Drunkenness. Sleep. These images describe people who are not prepared, people who are left vulnerable and wide open to the doom that is coming upon them. Darkness, drunkenness, and sleep leave us incapable of seeing, hearing, and responding to our surroundings. The only cure for darkness is light. The only cure for drunkenness is soberness. The only cure for being asleep is being awake.

Living in the light, living soberly, living wakefully—these terms describe the believer who sincerely and obediently follows Christ. Those who walk in the light can see and hear reality. They are alert and sensitive to the voice of God—and to spiritual danger.

Many years ago, an atheist farmer in Illinois sent a letter to the editor of the local weekly newspaper. He wrote:

> Sir:
>
> I have been trying an experiment. I have planted the field of corn, which I plowed on Sunday. I planted it on Sunday. I did all the cultivating which it received on Sunday. I gathered the crop on Sunday, and Sunday hauled it to my barn; and I find that I have more corn to the acre than has been gathered by any of my neighbors during this October.[18]

This atheist farmer had produced a bumper crop by working entirely on the Christian day of rest, and by doing so, he apparently believed he had disproved the existence of God. The newspaper editor published the letter word for word—but he added a brief editorial reply: "God does not always settle his accounts in October."

Many unbelievers think that living for self has made them successful.

Living without God or in defiance of God has made them rich. Living for wealth, fame, and power has given them everything they want in life. They are smug and self-satisfied—*in the October of their lives.*

But a day of reckoning is coming. From that day of judgment, there will be no escape. When Paul says, "destruction will come on them suddenly," he is not saying that unbelievers will be annihilated, that they will cease to exist. *They will exist*—but in a state of total separation from God. *They will exist*—but in a state of abject horror and regret for all they have lost. *They will exist*—but their existence will be too miserable to contemplate.

The destruction that overtakes them will make a killer tsunami look like a ripple on a pond, yet those who suffer that destruction will still exist in a state of spiritual awareness and despair. The book of Revelation tells us, "During those days people will seek death but will not find it; they will long to die, but death will elude them" (Revelation 9:6).

How can anyone escape from death to life, from spiritual darkness to spiritual light? There is only one way: Come to Christ while you still can. Turn to him and begin walking in his light today. Repent while there is still time—and still a way of salvation.

Jesus said, "I am the light of the world. Whoever follows me will never walk in darkness, but will have the light of life" (John 8:12). He can't put it more plainly than that.

THREE EVIDENCES THAT WE LIVE IN THE LIGHT

When the apostle Paul stood before King Agrippa and recounted his dramatic encounter with Christ on the road to Damascus, he said that God had specifically sent him to the Gentiles "to open their eyes and turn them from darkness to light, and from the power of Satan to God, so that they may receive forgiveness of sins" (Acts 26:18).

How do we truly know that we have been turned from darkness to light, from the power of Satan to God, from condemnation to the forgiveness of sins? There are three evidences in our lives that this transformation has taken place:

First, we have a *renewed character*.

Second, we have *radical conduct*.

Third, we have *reliable compensation*.

Let's look at each of these three evidences in turn.

First, *the evidence of a renewed character*. The difference between those who live in spiritual darkness and those who live in spiritual light is that the people of the light possess a radically different nature. We are not content to remain in our sin. Yes, we still sin, but when we sin, we cannot rest until we repent and turn from our sin and receive the Lord's forgiveness. We are like someone who was wearing a white garment, and the slightest stain bothers us and nags us until we cleanse that spot.

Those who are in spiritual darkness are like someone who is wearing a filthy garment. When your clothes are already filthy and stained, one more stain makes no difference. If you spill coffee on a grimy shirt, you won't even be able to find the stain—you'll shrug it off.

So it's important that we keep our spiritual garments clean and white at all times through confession, repentance, and receiving forgiveness. This process heightens our awareness of sin and makes us more sensitive to the conviction of the Holy Spirit. Paul calls this a state of being watchful and sober.

Believers who live in a state of moral and spiritual watchfulness have a renewed character. They continually renew their relationship with God by confessing their sins, repenting of sin, and being forgiven. Without that continual process of renewal, our relationship with God becomes distant and cold, and we lose our sensitivity to the Holy Spirit. To make sure that you have been moved from darkness to light, focus on maintaining your renewed character.

Second, *the evidence of radical conduct*. The Christian way of life is radical conduct by the world's standards. The people of this world don't know how to deal with us. They can't understand the Christian mindset. They don't understand how it is possible to love the sinner and hate the sin. So when we say, for example, that it is sin to engage in sexual relations outside of marriage, they falsely accuse us of being hateful toward people who engage in fornication, homosexuality, and adultery. The world doesn't understand that we condemn the sin *precisely because we love the sinner*, just as Jesus did. In John 8, when a group of evil men brought a woman before Jesus, accusing her of adultery and demanding that she be stoned to death, Jesus had compassion for her. She had sinned, but Jesus forgave her. Yet, he did not tell her (as our anything-goes culture today would tell her), "Off you go, enjoy your life of sin. If it feels good, do it." Instead, he told her, "Go now and leave your life of sin."

As Christians, following the example of our Lord, we live a radical lifestyle of confronting sin and loving sinners. The world calls us narrow-minded, intolerant bigots because we distinguish between truth and falsehood—and the world can't. We can distinguish between light and darkness—and the world can't. Jesus himself taught us how to balance grace and truth—but the world can't.

When we confront sin, such as sexual immorality or abortion, worldly people feel condemned, and they think *we* are condemning them. In reality, it's their own conscience that's burning. Their own conscience convicts them of their evil and darkness. Their own conscience reminds them of their rebellion against God. So they lash out at us in rage.

As Christians, we aren't morally superior to anyone else. We know we are merely sinners saved by grace. We don't hate anyone for being mired in their sins because we know that a life of sin is precisely what God in his grace has rescued us from. We didn't choose God, he chose us, and we have nothing to boast about except his amazing grace.

We are engaged in a great war—but the people of this world are not our enemies. We don't want to attack them, we want to enlist them in the spiritual battle against the invisible principalities and powers that have enslaved this world.

Our radical conduct is possible only when we are armed and armored for the battle. The apostle Paul put it this way: "But since we belong to the day, let us be sober, putting on faith and love as a breastplate, and the hope of salvation as a helmet" (5:8). We can tell that a believer is alert and prepared for battle by his armor.

An alert and ready Christian has put on faith and love like a flak vest (today's version of the ancient Roman breastplate). When we walk by faith, not by sight, we stand firm against the devil's schemes. Faith means trusting in God to keep his promises, believing in his Word even when the world is falling apart, relying on God's power as our defense against temptation, delighting in God's plan even when it doesn't make sense to us.

Paul says that we should not only put on faith but love as well. Love means putting the welfare of our fellow believers above our own. Love means accepting one another, deferring to one another, forgiving one another, and praying for one another.

So we put on faith and we put on love—the flak vest of our spiritual armor. Added to that, we put on the hope of salvation, which is the helmet that protects our life and our thoughts against attack. When we know we are saved, and we look forward to eternity in heaven with Jesus, we are protected against any head blows the enemy might try to inflict on us.

When you are attacked by the people of this world, remember that they are not the enemy. Remember who your real enemy is. Maintain a lifestyle of radical Christian conduct so that you can recruit the people around you in the good fight for the kingdom of God.

Third, *the evidence of reliable compensation.* Paul writes, "For God did not appoint us to suffer wrath but to receive salvation through our Lord Jesus Christ" (5:9). These Thessalonian believers were much like many Christians in our own day. They knew the Lord. They knew that they were saved. Yet they were afraid of the coming day of the Lord. Paul wanted them to know that our destiny, our reward, our compensation is real, it's certain, it's as dependable as the promises of God.

Some people will pass through physical death—which Paul refers to as "sleep"—before they meet the Lord face-to-face. Others will be alive, watching and waiting, when he returns, and they too will meet the Lord face-to-face. All believers will receive the reward of salvation—eternal life with Jesus.

The physical condition of the body doesn't matter. All that matters is the spiritual condition of the believer. Our reward is sure. Our compensation is reliable. "Therefore," Paul concludes, "encourage one another and build each other up, just as in fact you are doing" (5:11).

When should we encourage one another with the truth of our coming reward? At all times—and especially in times of discouragement.

When a husband and wife begin arguing over some silly and unimportant issue, they should encourage each other and remind each other of the great reward that awaits them.

Or you might hear a fellow Christian say, "The world is going insane. Our government is failing us. Our nation is hopelessly divided. The secularists are tearing down our culture. The terrorists are attacking us." Remind your discouraged friend that Jesus is coming and there is a great reward awaiting us.

When the church board is divided and bickering over some issue, whether it is a philosophy of ministry or the color of the carpet in the lobby, it's time to encourage one another and remind each other of the compensation that awaits all believers in Christ.

One of the great evangelists and revivalists of the nineteenth century was Charles G. Finney. Finney was preparing to become an attorney, studying law and working as an apprentice to a practicing attorney. One day, while alone in his office, he heard the Lord speaking to his heart.

"Finney," the Lord said, "what are you going to do when you complete your studies?"

"I'm going to put out a shingle and practice law."

"Then what will you do?"

"I'll get rich."

"Then what?"

"Retire comfortably."

"Then what?"

"Then—I'll die."

"Then what?"

Finney had never given that question much thought before. But as he struggled to answer it, he began to tremble. "Then," he said, "the day of judgment."

When Charles Finney spoke those words aloud, he came under such conviction that he leapt up from his desk, ran out of the building, and dashed into the woods. There, he knelt before God and invited the Lord Jesus Christ to take control of his life.

In the years that followed, the Lord used Charles G. Finney in a mighty way. He preached countless revival sermons and led many people to receive Christ or rededicate themselves to the Lord. He became a key figure in the abolitionist movement and the Underground Railroad, and he helped smuggle many escaped slaves to freedom in the North. He served as a professor and later president of Oberlin College in Ohio (which was originally founded as a Christian institution of higher learning).

What motivated Charles Finney to become an evangelist, a revivalist, an activist for the abolition of slavery, and a Christian educator? It all began when God confronted him with the day of judgment. It all began when Finney began to get serious with God about his eternal fate.

If you are not walking in the light with Christ—if you are still in the dark, still living for selfish goals, still living in rebellion or apathy toward the things of God—it's time for you to listen for the voice of God. He is asking you about your plan for your life, your death, and the afterlife.

You probably expect to die one day—but then again, you might be alive when Jesus returns like a thief in the night. But whether you are alive on that day or you die first, all your plans will one day come to a sudden halt. Listen to the voice of God. He's asking you, "Then what?"

I pray that you answer that question by receiving and serving him.

7

HOW TO BE THE CHURCH

1 Thessalonians 5:12-18

My late friend Chuck Colson once traveled to Japan with his wife, Patty. During a free afternoon, they visited what was reputed to be the fastest-growing "church" in the world. I say "church" in quotation marks because it was not a Christian church but a Buddhist congregation in Tokyo, the Perfect Liberty Church. Because nonmembers were not permitted inside the compound, Chuck and Patty could only peer through the gates.

The magnificent grounds included beautifully designed buildings, sculptured gardens, artificial lakes, waterfalls, and a sprawling golf course. The "church" could easily afford such opulent architecture and landscaping because its members were expected to give generously. Later, Chuck read a brochure that explained the "Perfect Liberty" philosophy, and then he turned to Patty and said, "They're saying that you can do whatever you want as long as it makes you happy. And they call that a church!"

After they returned to the States, Chuck and Patty were in a hotel room in Los Angeles, and they happened to watch a TV preacher and his wife, sitting in an opulent studio adorned with a stained-glass window, a black velvet portrait of Jesus, a white-and-gold baby grand piano. They listened in fascination and dismay to the prosperity gospel of these religious celebrities—a message Chuck summarized this way: "You can have perfect peace, joy, happiness, and prosperity. God wants no one to suffer or be deprived. Just ask. Ask and you will receive an abundance."

He later recalled that he had exactly the same reaction to this "televised travesty" as he had to the Buddhist "church" in Tokyo: "What nonsense. Imagine it! And they call *this* the church!" Chuck Colson later gave an interview in which he said:

> We have a scandalously low view of the church...We have been so suckered in by the radical individualism of American culture that we've stripped the church of its proper role. But God created the church for the redemption of humankind and to be a witness to the coming Kingdom... Despite the fact that 81 percent of the American people say they can find the truth about God without reference to church or synagogue, I now believe that you cannot live the Christian life apart from the church...
>
> Because evangelism is such a magnificent obsession for us, we tend to obscure the fullness of the Great Commission, which says we are to go and make disciples, baptizing and teaching them. That implies bringing people into the church, into a body.[19]

There can be no denying that, in recent decades, people have increasingly re-created the church in their own image—not in the image of Christ. They have refashioned the church according to their own likings and whims—not according to Scripture. I would go so far as to say that there are comparatively few truly biblical churches left.

Are we surprised, then, that the Christian church no longer has the impact on society it once had? Are we surprised that our society has turned increasingly against Christian beliefs and values? Are we surprised to find ourselves living in a post-Christian civilization?

WHAT THE CHURCH IS—AND ISN'T

For as long as the church has existed, there have been erroneous views of the church. In his last novel, *Ninety-Three* (1874), Victor Hugo wrote, "A church means the four walls within which the Almighty has his dwelling-place"[20]—as if Almighty God could be contained within the four walls of a building. Other people see the church as a prestigious social club, a charitable organization, or a denomination.

These notions about the church are utterly foreign to the Scriptures. The Greek word translated "church" appears more than a hundred times in the New Testament—and not once does it refer to a building or an institution or an organization or a denomination. Nowhere does the New Testament ever suggest that God makes his dwelling place between the four walls of a building.

Instead, the New Testament describes the church through a variety of metaphors. The church is a family, a gathering of our brothers and sisters in Christ. The church is a body, and Jesus is the head of the body. The church is a bride, and Christ is the loving and nurturing bridegroom.

Jesus himself defined the church in simple terms: "For where two or three gather in my name, there am I with them" (Matthew 18:20). This is the most basic and essential definition of the church: a gathering of two or more believers who come together in the Lord's name. Jesus does not even suggest that the gathering needs to have any purpose. Yes, we can gather together for worship or for ministry or for some other activity. But even if two believers gather together for blessed Christian fellowship, to bask in the pleasure of each other's Christian company, that is purpose enough—and those two believers are, by definition, the church.

Note that one important clause: "in my name." We must never neglect those three all-important words. Jesus, and Jesus alone, is our central focus. Jesus is the purpose for our existence as a church. Jesus is our sole object of worship. Jesus is our message. Jesus is our Center and our Focus. We are the church only when we come together *in the name of Jesus*.

If any other thing, any other person, any other agenda takes the place of Jesus, then we cease to be the church. As important as fellowship is, as important as preaching is, as important as music is, as important as outreach is, as important as missionary activities are, as important as our programs and ministries are, if Jesus is not our sole focus, then this gathering we call the church is falsely named. We are the church only if we are gathered *in his name*.

In the body of believers where I serve as pastor, I have seen people come and I have seen people go. They come for a variety of reasons— and they sometimes leave when their expectations aren't met. They may have wanted to hear a certain kind of message or a certain kind of music, or they might have wanted to experience a certain emotional thrill or spiritual high. When they failed to find it, they moved on.

Many churches market themselves like products. They try to appeal to the felt needs of their consumers. They are so busy promoting activities, programs, conferences, experiences, music, and excitement that Jesus—the One who is supposed to be central to everything—gets lost in the shuffle. All too many churches seem to have lost their focus on Jesus, and the result is that we now have a confused church culture.

The story is told of a man who was a castaway on a desert island. He managed to survive for two years before a ship came by and rescued him. His rescuers were surprised to discover that he had built three shacks on a hill. They asked him, "What are those three shacks for?"

"Well," he said, "the one in the middle is my house. And the one on the right side is my church."

"What about the shack on the left side?"

"Oh, that's the church I used to go to."

Does that sound familiar? Many Christians are church-hoppers. They find a church they like for a while, then something about that church offends them, so they hop to another church down the road and try that one for a while. In most cases, the problem is not with the church, it's with the church-hopper. These folks forget that the church is not about them and what they want. The church is about Jesus and what he wants.

The church is a gathering of God's people—but the church is not about the people. It's not about the pastor. It's not about the programs. It's not about the Sunday school or the youth program. No, the church is all about Jesus. And that's what the apostle Paul tells us in the next passage of this letter:

> Now we ask you, brothers and sisters, to acknowledge
> those who work hard among you, who care for you in the
> Lord and who admonish you. Hold them in the highest
> regard in love because of their work. Live in peace with
> each other. And we urge you, brothers and sisters, warn
> those who are idle and disruptive, encourage the disheart-
> ened, help the weak, be patient with everyone. Make sure
> that nobody pays back wrong for wrong, but always strive
> to do what is good for each other and for everyone else.
>
> Rejoice always, pray continually, give thanks in all circum-
> stances; for this is God's will for you in Christ Jesus (1 Thes-
> salonians 5:12-18).

This passage reveals four insights into the way God expects Christians to live together in this community called the church:

First, Paul urged the Thessalonians to value the preaching of the Word of God.

Second, Paul urged them to hold each other accountable for living productive, positive, compassionate, patient lives.

Third, he encouraged them to be forgiving toward one another, never paying back evil for evil.

Fourth, he exhorted them to always be rejoicing, praying, and giving thanks to God.

Let's take a closer look at each of these insights from the apostle Paul—insights into how to be the church of Jesus Christ.

1. VALUE THE PREACHING OF THE WORD

Paul instructed the Thessalonian believers to value the preaching of the Word of God. He urged them "to acknowledge those who work hard among you, who care for you in the Lord and who admonish you. Hold them in the highest regard in love because of their work."

Implicit in these words is an expectation that the leaders in the church would be diligent and hard-working. Hard-working doing what? Doing various kinds of social work? No! Paul said they were to work hard instructing the congregation. That's what "admonish" means.

What were they to instruct the people about? Sociology? Pop psychology? Improving their self-esteem? How to get rich? No! Pastors are to instruct the people in the Word of God and in the gospel of Jesus Christ.

I believe the New International Version inaccurately translates verse 12, where Paul says that believers ought to "acknowledge those who work hard among you, who care for you in the Lord and who admonish you." The original Greek phrase that the NIV translates "who care for you in the Lord" actually means "who are set over you in the Lord" or "who have authority over you in the Lord." Other translations, such as the King James Version, the English Standard Version, the Amplified Bible, and the New American Standard Bible all preserve the meaning of the original Greek language.

Paul is saying that God has entrusted pastors and elders in the church with responsibility and authority over the believers in the church. This doesn't mean that pastors are to lord it over the congregation or boss people around. No, their authority comes from the Word of God itself. That's the only authority a pastor has.

A minister of the gospel has a solemn responsibility to lift up the Word of God, to teach the Word with integrity and sincerity, to explain the Word diligently and with simplicity, and to exemplify the Word in every aspect of his private and public life. Whether a pastor is preaching a sermon, counseling an individual, solving a dispute, rebuking a wayward Christian, or encouraging a discouraged believer, everything that pastor says must be 100 percent consistent with the Word of God. Otherwise, that pastor is just offering his opinion, and one human opinion is essentially as good as another.

Paul said that a Christ-centered, biblically based, hard-working, truth-preaching leader in the church should be honored, loved, and respected because of his work for the Lord. This doesn't mean a pastor should be worshiped as if he were a Hollywood celebrity or the leader of a cult. This doesn't mean a pastor should be unaccountable or dictatorial. This doesn't mean that a pastor should never be confronted in love if he wanders from the truth.

This simply means that pastors deserve our respect and love. But only Jesus is to be worshiped. A faithful congregation puts Jesus first, and also values the faithful preaching of the Word of God.

From 1981 to 2013, Southern California's Crystal Cathedral was home to a Protestant church originally founded in 1955 by Dr. Robert H. Schuller. The late Dr. Schuller was a fine man, a minister in the Reformed Church in America—but Dr. Schuller decided that what people needed was a positive message that he called "possibility thinking." He envisioned preaching this message in a Crystal Cathedral, which was constructed of more than ten thousand rectangular panes of glass at a cost of $18 million—the largest all-glass building ever built. For years it was the setting of Dr. Schuller's weekly television ministry, *The Hour of Power*. By 2010, however, the church was deep in debt and filing for bankruptcy protection. In 2013, ownership of the building was transferred to the Roman Catholic Diocese of Orange, and the church was later reopened as a Catholic church called Christ Cathedral.

I don't fault Dr. Schuller's good intentions. And I believe he preached Christ from the pulpit of the Crystal Cathedral. But I don't think Christ was central to the message of the Crystal Cathedral. I think, without realizing it, Dr. Schuller gradually made "possibility thinking" the central focus of his preaching—and that is why the church ultimately failed.

In Chicago in 1864, while the American Civil War was still raging, evangelist Dwight L. Moody founded the Illinois Street Church. He founded that church on the good news of Jesus Christ. Mr. Moody died in 1899, but his successors were determined to maintain his commitment to preaching Christ. In 1925, they dedicated a new building in the Lincoln Park section of Chicago and named it the Moody Church in his honor. The Moody Church has never strayed from Mr. Moody's commitment to the purity of God's Word. Today, more than 150 years after its founding, the Moody Church is stronger than ever—and so is its commitment to the Word.

Faithfulness to the Word is key to the life and the longevity of the church. If we want the church to be alive and vibrant and effective a century from now (or until the Lord returns), we must value the preaching of the Word.

2. HOLD ONE ANOTHER ACCOUNTABLE

Paul urged the believers in Thessalonica to hold each other accountable for living productive, positive, compassionate, patient lives. There is no such thing as a perfect believer or a perfect church. If you ever find a perfect church, please don't join it—you'll only spoil it! And, of course, so would I. In fact, I can absolutely guarantee that as long as I am the pastor of my church, it will never be a perfect church!

We are all imperfect human beings, fallible and prone to sin—and that is why Christlike love is so important in the church. Because we are imperfect, we must learn to accept one another and tolerate one another in all our many imperfections. Because we are imperfect, we must learn to love one another with genuine *agape* love. Because we are imperfect, we must learn to forgive one another. And because we are imperfect, we must hold one another accountable.

The culture around us embraces a false notion of tolerance and love that says, "If you love somebody, you have to accept all their sins, their character flaws, and their godless lifestyle. You must never correct them, never rebuke them, never challenge them, never encourage them to repent and live righteously. Love means tolerating whatever anyone does, including their sinful and destructive behavior."

That's the world's notion of love—and if you violate that notion, if you confront or rebuke someone for a lifestyle of sin, suddenly you will become the bad guy, the bigot, the hater, the reactionary, the extremist. According to the world, the out-and-proud sinners are good, and the godly are evil. Right is wrong and wrong is right. We are living in Orwellian times.

But God's Word teaches that admonishing one another in a spirit of humility is actually a demonstration of Christian love. As someone once said, "If you love, you level." Paul calls this "speaking the truth in love" (Ephesians 4:15). Paul is not telling us to go around and correct and confront our fellow Christians for every little thing they do wrong.

But if someone is straying from the truth or wandering from the faith, if someone is engaging in a lifestyle of sin and self-destruction, we should love that person enough to sit down, reason, pray, and even weep with that person over the tragedy of sin. That's what it truly means to love one another.

Paul encourages believers to warn those who are idle—those who are lazy and unproductive. They're capable of working, yet they sponge off their Christian brothers and sisters instead.

He also says to warn the "disruptive." This word comes from a military context and refers to a soldier who is found guilty of disorderly conduct. A soldier who will not carry out his duties and responsibilities is worse than useless—his lack of discipline is a threat to his fellow soldiers and the war effort. In a church, a disruptive "Christian soldier" undermines the unity and ministry of the church.

Paul also says that we are to encourage the disheartened, the worried and anxious, the troubled and timid, those who are frightened for their safety. This was important in the early church because there was rampant persecution against the church. Believers needed to be continually reminded of the promises and protection of God. We may see increasing persecution of the church in our own culture in the twenty-first century. When that persecution comes, we will need to encourage the disheartened all the more.

Next, Paul says, "help the weak, be patient with everyone." Many in the church are emotionally and spiritually fragile. They are easily beset with doubt. We need to remind them of the rewards of faith. We need to remind them that the Lord could return at any time, and he will take us home to heaven to be with him forevermore.

We need to be patient with those who are weak, those who lack a strong faith or a strong character. Often, those who are weak and timid have suffered emotional wounds. Sometime in the past, they might have been mighty spiritual warriors—but some traumatic experience, some deep loss, some yet-unhealed wound has left them spiritually shell-shocked. Be kind, be compassionate, be patient with them—just as the Lord has been patient with you.

As members of the body of Christ, we will sometimes be called upon to hold each other accountable—and at other times to encourage each other with patient words of grace.

3. BE FORGIVING, NOT VENGEFUL

Paul urged the believers in Thessalonica to be forgiving toward one another, never taking revenge. "Make sure that nobody pays back wrong for wrong," he wrote, "but always strive to do what is good for each other and for everyone else" (5:15).

There are many differences between Islam and Christianity, but one of the most striking centers on the issue of vengeance. Muslims are taught that they have a duty to avenge their god, Allah. If anyone insults Allah, a Muslim is morally obligated to defend Allah's name by taking revenge against the blasphemer.

But the Bible takes the opposite view. In the Scriptures, we are not taught to avenge God. Rather, God says he is the One who will avenge us! We are not to exact vengeance against anyone. Instead, God says, "It is mine to avenge; I will repay" (Deuteronomy 32:35; Romans 12:19).

Moreover, Jesus tells us in the Sermon on the Mount that we are to love our enemies and pray for those who hurt us and abuse us. And Paul, quoting from the book of Proverbs, writes:

> "If your enemy is hungry, feed him;
>   if he is thirsty, give him something to drink.
> In doing this, you will heap burning coals on his head."
>   (Romans 12:20)

Many of us would like to skip the part about giving our enemy food and drink and go straight to those burning coals! But God is telling us that by showing kindness to wrongdoers, we may actually cause their consciences to burn—and they may repent of their wrongdoing and even turn to God for salvation.

And let's face it—not all the hurts we suffer come from the ungodly and the unsaved. Very often, we suffer attacks, false accusations, gossip, and other wounds from our fellow Christians. When we are harmed by someone in the body of Christ, it hurts even more than a wound from an unbeliever. We *trust* other Christians to love us, to accept us, and to think the best of us. It feels like a betrayal when a fellow Christian rejects us, attacks us, and thinks the worst.

Paul said we should all live lives of love and forgiveness, always doing what is good for each other, never holding grudges, never getting even. If everyone in the church lived out this simple principle, the body of Christ would become an unbelievably powerful force in our culture. We would be truly united in Christian love, and the world around us would be convicted and changed by the power of our Christlike example.

Both within the church and outside the church, let's leave vengeance to God. When it comes to avenging sin, God knows exactly what he's doing. We can trust him to get it right every time.

4. REJOICE, PRAY, AND BE THANKFUL

Paul writes, "Rejoice always, pray continually, give thanks in all circumstances; for this is God's will for you in Christ Jesus" (5:16-18). You and I both know that we don't always feel like rejoicing. We don't always feel like praying. And we certainly don't always feel thankful. So what do we do with Paul's command to rejoice always, pray continually, and give thanks in all circumstances? Is the Bible hopelessly unrealistic? Or is this truly practical advice for Christian living?

First, how can we rejoice always? It's important to remember that the apostle Paul was no Pollyanna. He knew what it meant to suffer persecution, opposition, rejection, and slander. Paul never exhorted us to be happy at all times. Instead, he said we should "rejoice always." He was telling us that, even in unhappy circumstances, we can experience joy.

You see, there's a big difference between happiness and joy. Happiness is based on our circumstances. When life is going well, when the sun is shining, when the economy is humming along, when our bills are paid, when life is good, we are happy. But when catastrophe strikes, when the storm rolls in, when the economy tanks, when there's too much month at the end of the money, then life turns sour and we become unhappy. That's normal. That's to be expected.

But joy is independent of our circumstances. We can be in trouble, facing a major illness or a devastating loss, and we can still have joy. We may not be giddy with happiness, but instead of focusing on our unhappy circumstances, we turn our eyes toward God and we focus on his love, his promises, his presence, his peace that passes all understanding. And in the midst of those unhappy circumstances, we have joy.

Let me suggest ten reasons for having joy all the time, regardless of how painful your circumstances may be:

1. You can rejoice always in God's righteous character.
2. You can rejoice always in God's redeeming love.
3. You can rejoice always in the Holy Spirit's comforting ministry to you.
4. You can rejoice always in the gifts and the blessings of the Holy Spirit.
5. You can rejoice always in God's promise to work all things together for good.
6. You can rejoice always in anticipation of your coming reward in heaven.
7. You can rejoice always in prayers God has answered in the past.
8. You can rejoice always in the gift of God's Word.
9. You can rejoice always in God's ever-present fellowship with you.
10. You can rejoice always because God will be glorified even through your difficult circumstances.

So rejoice always.

Second, what does it mean to pray without ceasing? Biblical prayer is a multidimensional experience with God. Unfortunately, all too many

Christians have a prayer life that is purely one-dimensional. Using a musical metaphor, their prayers consist of a single note, played over and over and over again. That note is petition—asking God for something.

There's nothing wrong with a prayer of petition. On many occasions throughout the Gospels, Jesus urges us to ask God to supply our needs. But we should not neglect all the other dimensions of prayer. Authentic biblical prayer encompasses all these dimensions:

- submission of our will to God's will
- praise to God—recognition of his glory, righteousness, power, and love
- thanksgiving to God for all he has done for us, especially our salvation
- confession and repentance
- intercession—asking God to meet the needs of other people
- petition—asking God to meet our needs

When Paul tells us that we should "pray continually," he is telling us that we should live our lives in a continual attitude of prayer. Our thoughts and our speech should be a running conversation with God and a continuous recognition that he is always present with us.

You wake up in the morning and you praise God for his goodness and thank him for a new day in which to serve him. Over breakfast and coffee, you thank him for food and drink. You hear about a natural disaster in the news or you receive a distressing email from a friend, and you immediately ask God to help those people and meet those needs. At work, you lose your temper with a coworker, and you immediately confess your sin to God, and then ask your coworker's forgiveness. Later in the day, your spouse phones and says a letter arrived from the IRS—you're being audited. If you're in an attitude of continual prayer, you won't swear. You'll petition God for wisdom and help.

The believer who prays continually has a continuous desire to glorify God in prayer. That believer will drink deeply of fellowship with God. That believer will trust God implicitly to meet every need through prayer. That believer will continually seek God's wisdom in prayer. That believer will seek God's strength and deliverance from temptation through prayer. That believer will unload all worries and anxieties through prayer. That believer will confess each sin and renew a right relationship with God through prayer. That believer will seek opportunities to share the good news through prayer.

This is how we transform an occasional ritual of prayer into a perpetual habit of prayer. Instead of occasionally "saying a prayer," we find ourselves inhaling and exhaling prayer just as we inhale and exhale the oxygen that sustains us. We never really stop praying—the conversation with God, both speaking to God and listening to God, just goes on and on. That is how we pray without ceasing.

Third, what does Paul mean when he says "give thanks in all circumstances"? For most of our society, the word *thanksgiving* means nothing more than a secular holiday of feasting and football. But when President George Washington proclaimed the first Thanksgiving in 1789, and when President Abraham Lincoln proclaimed Thanksgiving to be a federal holiday in 1863, that day was set aside as a day of remembering God's blessings and offering prayers of gratitude to our Creator.

It is only natural that Paul adds thanksgiving to rejoicing and praying. These three spiritual habits go together. When we are continually in tune with God, these three activities form the natural rhythms of our lives. You may not always feel happy, but you can always rejoice in the presence of God. You may not always feel strong and confident, but you can always pray for strength and wisdom. You may not always experience pleasant circumstances, but you can give thanks for your salvation in all circumstances, pleasant or otherwise.

Many Christians have misunderstood Paul's counsel to "give thanks in all circumstances." There is a world of difference between being thankful *in* our circumstances versus being thankful *for* our circumstances. If you receive a cancer diagnosis or if your house burns down, God does not expect you to go to him and say, "Lord, thank you for my cancer," or "Lord, thank you that I lost everything in the fire."

We can't always be thankful *for* our circumstances—but we can always be thankful *in* our circumstances. We can be thankful that God is present with us. We can be thankful for his promises. We can be thankful for Christian friends who support us and pray for us. We can be thankful that God is doing a work in our lives that we cannot understand as yet. Even amid our crises and calamities, there are things we can be thankful for.

Paul tells us, "Rejoice always, pray continually, give thanks in all circumstances; for this is God's will for you in Christ Jesus." Believing that God's will is being perfected in our lives day by day, we are able to rejoice regardless of our emotions, pray regardless of our weakness, and give thanks regardless of our circumstances. That is God's will for you and me.

UNCOMMON CHRISTIANS

Henry W. Frost (1858–1945) was a missionary to China during the early twentieth century, serving with Hudson Taylor's China Inland Mission. He once wrote an essay for CIM titled "Uncommon Christians." There he described an "uncommon Christian" as a believer who:

1. makes God's Word his only, his full, and his constant rule of faith and practice

2. lives out his life, having no confidence in the flesh, but having all confidence in the person and power of the Holy Spirit

3. makes the Lord Jesus Christ once and forever the absolute Lord of his life

4. has the vision of those who walk in heavenly places, and who thus sees things from the heavenly and larger standpoint

5. gives his life irrevocably to God for the saving and sanctifying of the souls of men.[21]

That is one of the best and most complete descriptions ever penned of the kind of person a Christian should be. But even an uncommon

Christian is only flesh and blood, and once, while Henry Frost was serving on the mission field, he underwent a trial of soul-deep darkness and depression. He described his experience in these words:

> I had received sad news from home, and deep shadows had covered my soul. I prayed, but the darkness did not vanish. I summoned myself to endure, but the darkness only deepened. Then I went to an inland station and saw on the wall of the mission home these words: TRY THANKSGIVING. I did, and in a moment every shadow was gone, not to return. Yes, the psalmist was right. "It is good to give thanks to the Lord."[22]

Whatever emotions you're feeling right now, however doubtful and uncertain you may feel about the road ahead, however weak and weary you may feel, whatever the circumstances you face, God is with you. He wants the best for you, and he is summoning the best from you.

You are his child, you are part of his church, and you have a part to play in his eternal plan for human history. Play your part. Be an uncommon Christian. Rejoice always, pray continually, and in all circumstances, try thanksgiving.

8

THE POWER AND
THE PROMISES

1 Thessalonians 5:19-28

B ritish inventor Joseph Swan began the commercial production of electric lightbulbs in 1881. Around that time, the first electric power company in Great Britain began illuminating the Holborn district of central London, including the general post office and the City Temple Church.

Queen Victoria, however, steadfastly refused to permit the electrification of Windsor Castle, except in a few public rooms that she rarely visited except on state occasions. By the time of her death in 1901, most of England was illuminated by electricity—but not Windsor Castle. Journalist Fiona Ross records that Queen Victoria "was naturally frugal, a hoarder and creature of habit; Victoria only ever used wax candles to light her rooms."[23]

Queen Victoria was one of the wealthiest and most powerful rulers in history, reigning over a British Empire that encircled the globe, from the British Isles to India to Australia to Canada. She could have made Windsor Castle shine through the night with an electric gleam, but for twenty years she chose to spend her nights in a smoky candlelit twilight because she was too frugal to spend a few pennies a month for electricity. The power was available—but the queen refused to plug into it.

I see Queen Victoria as a metaphor of the way many Christians live.

17

All the vast globe-spanning power of the kingdom of God is at our disposal—yet we choose to live by dim, flickering candlelight, ignoring the brilliant, illuminating power that could so easily be ours. We are already wired by God to receive that power, yet we refuse to tap into it. That's why so many Christians seem to live in a spiritual twilight when they could be rejoicing in the electrifying power of the Spirit of God.

If you would like to discover how to put away your spiritual candles and plug into the high-voltage adventure that God has planned for you, read on.

DON'T DOUSE THE FIRE!

In the closing verses of Paul's first letter to the Thessalonians, the apostle begins with a brief yet profound statement about the Holy Spirit:

Do not quench the Spirit (1 Thessalonians 5:19).

Paul uses an interesting turn of phrase—*quenching the Holy Spirit*—when he speaks of those who fail to tap into God's limitless power for their lives. To quench is to extinguish, as in quenching a fire. If you are camping in the woods, and you are about to leave your campsite, it's important to quench any smoldering embers in your campfire pit. Otherwise, sparks could fly and ignite a forest fire. That's sensible.

But it would be foolish to quench a campfire while you're still cooking your pot of beans. You need the power of that fire to heat your dinner. Yet that is exactly what many Christians do—they quench the fire of the Holy Spirit, throwing cold water on the power of the Spirit right when they need it most.

The Spirit is still present—but they choose to live by human-centered answers. The Spirit still indwells them—but they neglect to listen to his voice. The Spirit still makes his power available to them for the asking—but they choose to live each day by the dim and partial light of their own understanding.

That's why so many believers lack discernment and wisdom. That's why so many believers are unable to understand and apply the Word of God in their daily lives. That's why so many believers are confused over what is true and what is false, what is right and what is wrong. Instead of living by the limitless power of the Holy Spirit, they operate according to their own opinions and common sense—then they wonder why they keep making disastrous decisions.

So Paul gives the believers in Thessalonica a series of exhortations, beginning with, "Do not quench the Spirit." He will follow this statement by urging Christians not to despise the Word of God, but to examine everything carefully, holding tightly to what is good and rejecting whatever is evil. But "Do not quench the Spirit" comes first because this is the key to everything that comes afterward. In order to live wisely, in order to understand God's Word, in order to discern what is good from what is evil, we need the power and illumination that comes from the Spirit. If we quench the Spirit, everything Paul tells us after that becomes nonsense.

Paul wants us to plug into the power of the Spirit and to allow the high voltage of God's wisdom to surge through us, enlightening our minds and illuminating our lives. Paul is not saying for a moment that we can actually turn off the power of the Holy Spirit at the Source. The Spirit of God himself can never be extinguished. But we can cut ourselves off from that eternal flame, and that is the quenching Paul warns us against.

When we receive Jesus as our Lord and Savior, he comes to indwell us with a fire that glows, with a light that shines, with a power that radiates, with a heat that purges and purifies. But God does not overrule our free will. You and I can dim the light and dial back the power of God's Spirit in our lives.

How do we quench God's Spirit? We quench the Spirit by allowing ungodly thoughts to dwell in us and build strongholds in our minds. We quench the Spirit by allowing our emotions to be infiltrated by ungodly affections. We quench the Spirit by allowing our beliefs and values to be infected by the false notions of this dying world. We quench the Spirit by allowing our decisions to be influenced by unchristian motives.

When we stop listening to the Spirit and begin listening to our own will, our own lusts, and the deceptive messages of our post-Christian culture, we douse the Spirit's fire within us. We become rebellious and self-willed. We become critical and unrighteous. We become bitter and angry. We become focused on selfish ambitions and godless desires. And we dampen the fire of the Holy Spirit in our lives.

I want to make sure that no one misunderstands what I'm saying. I am *absolutely not* saying that a believer can lose the Holy Spirit. The Bible does not teach that a believer can lose the Holy Spirit. What I *am* saying is what the Bible teaches—that we can individually cause the power of the Holy Spirit in us to be doused. The Spirit still indwells us, is still available to us, still pleads with us, and still loves us—but we have flipped a switch and turned off the power.

We are like Windsor Castle in the days of Queen Victoria. There were power lines running from the power station to the castle, and those power lines were connected to lightbulbs in a few rooms in the public section of the castle. But the queen refused to permit the wiring to be extended to her living quarters. Vast power was available to her, but by her own choice, she chose instead the dim and flickering candles. The Holy Spirit is always available to believers, if we will choose to tap into the Spirit's limitless power. It is our choice—and ours alone—that limits the Holy Spirit's power in our lives.

If you have ever tried to read a book by candlelight during a power blackout, you know that the dim and flickering flame provides poor illumination for reading. I would prefer a bright, steady 100-watt bulb any day. Bright light makes a book easier to read and easier to understand. In the same way, the illuminating power of the Holy Spirit makes the Bible plain and understandable. Trying to grasp God's Word by reading by the dim and flickering candle flame of our human understanding is simply foolish, especially when the brilliant light of God is available for the asking.

The Holy Spirit wants to guide our steps and help us to make wise decisions—but if we quench the flame of the Spirit, we will wander in darkness and invite disaster. The Holy Spirit wants to give us the power to overcome temptation—but if we quench the flame of the Spirit, we leave ourselves wide open to Satan's deception. The Holy Spirit wants to open the eyes of our spiritual understanding—but if we quench the flame of the Spirit, we remain willfully blind and ignorant of reality.

We quench the Spirit when we insist on clinging to our pride and our confidence in our own strength. We quench the Spirit when we cling to sin and unforgiveness. We quench the Spirit when we replace the wisdom of the Word of God with our human folly. And we should be aware that not only can individuals quench the Spirit, but entire churches can quench the Spirit. Many churches today exhibit great pride and self-confidence, tolerate sin and practice unforgiveness, and have replaced God's Word with human ideas and programs.

When individual believers and entire congregations quench the Spirit, disaster will follow as surely as the night follows the day. So Paul's counsel, "Do not quench the Spirit," is as timely today as when he first wrote those simple-yet-profound words.

PUT EVERYTHING TO THE TEST

With that urgent counsel as his foundation, Paul goes on to write:

> Do not treat prophecies with contempt but test them all; hold on to what is good, reject every kind of evil (1 Thessalonians 5:20-22).

Here Paul urges all believers to treat the Word of God with respect, to examine every doctrine and belief carefully, to hold tightly to what is good and to reject everything that is evil.

In our church, the leaders meet regularly, both throughout the week and on Sunday mornings between services, and they join their hearts to pray one prayer: "Holy Spirit, move freely in our midst with all your power—and anything that gets in your way, up to and including the preacher, remove it." That is the prayer of our church because we do not want to quench the Holy Spirit, and we do not want anything or anyone to get in the way of the Word of God. We want the Word to go forth from our church with life-changing, world-changing power.

Paul follows this teaching with an equally urgent command not to despise the Word of God. This is a natural sequence. If the Holy

Spirit is quenched, then a disregard for God's Word soon follows. What does it mean to treat the prophecies of God's Word with contempt? It means to minimize God's Word, to hold it in disregard, to consider it as unimportant and having no authority over our lives. Today, many churches claim to uphold the Word of God while treating its teachings with contempt.

Many churches have tried to circumvent the Bible's clear and unmistakable teachings about salvation by grace through faith, the sanctity of life, the sanctity of marriage, the warnings against becoming unequally yoked with irreligion or false religion, and the reality of Satan and hell and eternal judgment. These clear biblical teachings are disregarded—and therefore held in contempt—by many churches today. Those churches have placed a higher priority on political correctness and friendship with the world than they have on the authority of Scripture. They would never openly criticize Scripture—they just quietly sweep certain passages and principles under the rug and hope nobody notices.

But God notices. When the church disregards the Word of God, which was delivered to us by his faithful prophets and apostles, there is always a price to pay. The canon of the Word of God is complete and the teachings of the Word of God are reliable. We do not need any new revelation from God. We simply need to listen to what he has already revealed to us in his Word. That is the Word Paul warns us not to treat with contempt.

Moreover, Paul tells us that we must examine everything—our individual decisions, our church ministry, our political and social views, our decisions in the voting booth, the books we read and the television shows we watch, the messages we post on social media—all must be evaluated in the light of God's Word. "Test them all," he writes. "Hold on to what is good, reject every kind of evil." Test everything by exposing it to the white-hot light of the Word of God.

How well do you understand the world around you? How wide is your knowledge? How deep is your wisdom? Make sure that everything you know and believe and think has been tested against the Word of God. Make sure you cling to God's truth, not merely your own opinions.

But how can we test everything in the light of God's Word if we have dampened the power of the Holy Spirit in our lives? How can we distinguish truth from falsehood unless we invite the Spirit to shed his light on our understanding? Paul's logical progression is inexorable. We can plainly see why our first priority is to make sure we do not quench the Holy Spirit.

A few years ago, a prominent minister wrote a bestselling book on the Holy Spirit. It sold millions of copies. Throughout the book, this minister referred to the Holy Spirit as "it," not "he." To the undiscerning, this may seem like a small matter. But by depersonalizing the Holy Spirit, this man presented to his readers a false picture of God. He made it easy for people to get the impression that God is not truly a Person. In fact, it is becoming popular in certain circles to suggest that God is nothing more than an "impersonal force" or a "creative principle" or a "moral imperative."

After that book hit the bestseller lists, another Christian leader went to that minister and confronted him in the spirit of Ephesians 4:15—"speaking the truth in love." He showed this man that, throughout the Bible (at least, in the original languages), the Holy Spirit is always referred to with the masculine pronoun *he*.[24] After this minister was corrected, he publicly apologized for his error, saying that he had never been to seminary so was not aware of how the Holy Spirit was referred to in the original Bible manuscripts.

It's embarrassing to have to apologize for a major error in a book—especially a bestseller. It's important to examine everything against Scripture, in reliance on the wisdom of the Holy Spirit. Our generation is desperate for the discernment and insight that can come only by tapping into the inexhaustible power of the Spirit.

During Paul's second missionary journey, after he escaped from Thessalonica, he went next to the northern Greek city of Berea. There Paul preached the gospel to the Berean Jews, teaching them about the Messiah from the Old Testament prophecies. Acts tells us that the Bereans "received the message with great eagerness and examined the Scriptures every day to see if what Paul said was true. As a result, many of them believed" (Acts 17:11-12).

If these Bereans were examining the Scriptures to see if what the apostle Paul said was true—that is, consistent with the Old Testament prophecies—then we also need to test the preaching we hear against the standard of God's Word. We should never take the message in any sermon or Christian book at face value. We should always make sure that what a minister or author says squares with the Word of God.

When we test a message, a book, or a doctrine against the objective standard of God's Word, one of two things will happen. Either we will find that the message, book, or doctrine is consistent with the Bible—or it is not. Paul says that we should "hold on to what is good" and "reject every kind of evil."

If you take large-denomination paper money to a bank, the bank officials will examine that money carefully. They will test it by holding it up to the light and examining it under magnification. They will determine whether that money is authentic or counterfeit. They will hold on to money that is good, and they will reject money that is false. That is how we should treat any notion or idea that claims to be the truth.

When you hear a teaching that you know violates the authentic Word of God, then it doesn't matter how well-intentioned the teacher might be, you must reject that teaching. When you hear a sermon that claims to be rooted in the Word of God, and upon examination you find that it resonates with the Scriptures, then hold on to that message. Learn from it. Believe it. Apply it to your life.

When you are plugged into the illuminating power of the Holy Spirit, you will recognize whether someone is expounding the Word of God or spouting psychobabble. Make sure you receive the Word and reject the babble.

Unfortunately, all too many people today fall for messages that are entertaining and appeal to their fallen nature and their flesh. They seek out a message that makes them feel good about who they are as sinners, rather than seeking a message that challenges them to repent and submit to God.

Some of the false gospels rampant in our society today contain just enough truth to sound plausible—even to seem biblical. But please remember this: A message that is "almost right" is wrong. A message that is "almost true" is false. In fact, a message that is a subtle distortion of the truth may be far more dangerous than an outright lie because it is more likely to lead people astray.

It has been said that error always rides on the back of truth. There is a deceptive sales technique known as "bait and switch." As an advertiser, you offer a product at a ridiculously low price to bait people into coming into the store. When they arrive, you inform them that the product they want is out of stock (fact is, it is *always* out of stock), and then you switch them to another product that is inferior—and more expensive.

Many preachers and bestselling authors use a similar bait-and-switch approach in peddling their false gospels. They use pious-sounding language, they quote verses of Scripture (wrenched out of context), they surround their message with Christian music—and when you are ready to buy what they are selling, they switch you to a false gospel.

Don't fall for a bait-and-switch gospel. Don't be deceived. Test every sermon you hear, every Christian book you read (including this one) by the objective standard of God's Word. Hold on to what is good, reject every kind of evil.

PAUL'S PRAYER

Finally, Paul concludes his letter with a subject that most Christians find convicting and challenging—the subject of prayer. He writes:

> May God himself, the God of peace, sanctify you through and through. May your whole spirit, soul and body be kept blameless at the coming of our Lord Jesus Christ. The one who calls you is faithful, and he will do it.
>
> Brothers and sisters, pray for us. Greet all God's people with a holy kiss. I charge you before the Lord to have this letter read to all the brothers and sisters.
>
> The grace of our Lord Jesus Christ be with you (1 Thessalonians 5:23-28).

Earlier, we saw that Paul urged believers to "pray continually," and we saw what that means in practical terms. Now Paul urges us to pray by interceding for others, and he instructs us in how to pray for them.

First, he offers a prayer for the Thessalonian believers that God would "sanctify you through and through." What does this mean? Sanctification, as we have already seen, means to be set apart for God's use. Paul is praying that the Thessalonian Christians would become more and more like Christ, more and more set apart for ministry, and more and more separated from sin.

John the Baptist put it this way: "He must become greater; I must become less" (John 3:30)—or as the King James Version beautifully expresses it, "He must increase, but I must decrease." John the Baptist desired to get himself, his personality, his ego, his sins out of the way so that Christ could be made manifest. He desired that there would be less of John the Baptist and more of Jesus the Messiah.

That is my prayer every day—that there would be less of Michael Youssef and more of Christ. This process of sanctification in my life must continue to go forward, day by day, until there is ultimately no more of Michael and everything of Christ.

As you pray for your own sanctification, and intercede for the sanctification of others, remember the three elements of our sanctification: past, present, and future. In the *past*, when we came to Christ, God sanctified us by securing our *positional sanctification*. Hebrews 10:10 tells us that "we have been made holy through the sacrifice of the body of Jesus Christ *once for all*." In the past, we were sanctified through salvation, and that can never be taken away from us.

But we are also sanctified in the *present*. That is, we are daily being sanctified. With each passing day, we grow in our character. God uses all the experiences of our lives to conform us into the image of Christ. As we surrender to this process of sanctification, the Spirit is able to empower us to become less like us and more like Christ.

Finally, we are sanctified in the *future*. This is the ultimate sanctification, the pinnacle of being set apart for God. It takes place when the Lord makes each of us sinless like himself. He makes us perfect in body, spirit, and soul.

Paul's prayer for the Thessalonians—and for all believers, including you and me—is that we would daily decrease so that Christ may daily increase in us. God is not satisfied with our partial sanctification. As Paul writes, God wishes us to be sanctified "through and through." Christ, living in us, must completely take over every part of our lives. We must come to a point where we can honestly say, "Not an inch of my life is withheld from the Lord's control. I am completely submitted to him."

That's what Paul means when he says, "We take captive every thought to make it obedient to Christ" (2 Corinthians 10:5). Sanctification cannot begin on the outside. It must begin within us, at the level of our thoughts, then radiate outward to our actions. Sanctification is an inside job. It starts deep within the soul and spirit, and then it moves to the body.

Your spirit is the most distinct and individual part of you. It's the dimension of you that connects with the Holy Spirit when you come to Christ. When the Holy Spirit dwells in your spirit, then your body will respond in obedience.

The ancient Greeks thought that the body is evil but the soul is good. So they let their bodies be involved in all sorts of immorality. As long as they were thinking lofty thoughts, they could do whatever they wanted with their bodies. It's a compartmentalized way of thinking—and it's completely unbiblical.

The Scriptures present an *integrated* view of our humanity. Yes, there is a spirit dimension, a soul dimension, and a physical dimension to our being—but we don't compartmentalize these different parts of ourselves, and we don't dismiss one dimension as less important than any other. The Word of God teaches that our thoughts produce our actions, and our body is no less important than our soul and spirit. In fact, the Scriptures tell us that the body is the temple of the Holy Spirit.

CHANGE BEGINS WITHIN

In the late 1950s, behavioral psychologist B.F. Skinner taught that human free will is an illusion and the only way to improve human behavior was through a system of rewards and punishment called "behavior modification." He continued to promote these notions well into the 1970s. But psychologists and psychiatrists and sociologists who tried to implement his ideas found that they failed again and again. By the late 1980s, behavior modification had fallen into disfavor for the simple reason that it doesn't work. The behaviorists were looking at the problem through the wrong end of the telescope.

If you want to change people for the better, you have to start within—at the level of the mind, the heart, and the will. These inward aspects of our being must be sanctified and set apart for God. When our inner being becomes holy, our behavior will follow. When the seed is righteous, the tree will bring forth good fruit.

How do we become righteous? Is it a matter of human effort, will-power, and trying harder to be good? No. Righteousness comes only from God. As Paul says, "The one who calls you is faithful, and he will do it." Our job is to live in total dependence upon him.

We have no reason to be confident in our own efforts. Our confidence is in the faithfulness of God. We can trust God completely because he always keeps his promises and he always finishes what he starts. The power of God is inextricably connected with the promises of God.

I am reminded of this principle every time parents dedicate their children to the Lord in front of the congregation. In front of all those witnesses, they are covenanting with God to bring their children up in the nurture and admonition of the Lord. I often remind them that what they are doing is more than merely a dedication. They are actually saying to God, "We have every confidence that, no matter what the future may bring, no matter what circumstances our children may go through, you, God, will see to it that they come to know you. Even if you have to drag them kicking and screaming into your fold, we have confidence in your faithfulness, Lord. You are faithful, and you will do it."

Finally, Paul concluded his letter with a plea that the Thessalonian believers would pray for him and his partners in ministry—and in return, he offered a prayer for them. Paul's closing prayer is also my prayer for you before we turn the page and look at Paul's second letter to the Thessalonians: "The grace of our Lord Jesus Christ be with you."

9

THE END OF HISTORY

2 Thessalonians 1:1-4

O ne of automaker Henry Ford's most famous quotations is "History is bunk." Ironically, Ford had a huge nostalgic fondness for the past, and in 1929, he opened an eighty-acre outdoor museum, the Henry Ford Museum and Greenfield Village, which preserves Thomas Edison's laboratory, the Wright Brothers' bicycle shop, the home where Noah Webster composed the first American dictionary, and the building where Abraham Lincoln practiced law.

It wasn't history itself—the actual span of human lives and human endeavors—that Ford considered bunk. What he dismissed was the history recorded in history books, consisting primarily of kings and generals and the dates of the wars they fought.

Before he opened his museum, he wrote to a friend, "We're going to build a museum that's going to show industrial history, and it won't be bunk! We'll show the people what actually existed in years gone by and we'll show the actual development of American industry from the early days...up to the present day."[25]

Ford had little use for the history found in history books, because it didn't tell the story of how ordinary people make extraordinary contributions to the world. There's something to be said for Henry Ford's view of history.

But the day is coming when even Ford's broader definition of history will end up on the ash heap. Henry Ford failed to understand that there is an even deeper historical record that is woven into the fabric of time and space. It began at the moment of creation, when a Voice spoke to the darkness, "Let there be light!" And that long scroll of history will come to an end with the establishment of the New Jerusalem by the One who said, "I am the Alpha and the Omega, the First and the Last, the Beginning and the End" (Revelation 22:13).

In the final analysis, the only true and meaningful history is His Story.

It's the story of the God who calls himself "the God of Abraham, Isaac, and Jacob." It's the story of the God who chose Israel out of all the nations of the earth to be his covenant people. It's the story of how God invested two thousand years in preparing the Israelites for the fulfillment of his promise to Abraham—the coming of the Messiah. And it's the story of how God came among us as a baby, born of a virgin, who grew in wisdom and stature, who preached the good news of the kingdom, who suffered under Pontius Pilate, was crucified and buried, and on the third day rose again. It's the story of how, at the appointed time in history, he sent his Holy Spirit. And it's the story of how his followers have been commissioned to take the good news of Jesus Christ to the ends of the earth.

That is His Story. That is history.

And when that task is accomplished, when the Great Commission has been fulfilled, when the gospel has been preached throughout the world as a testimony to all nations, history will come to an end.

That is not my opinion. That is what Jesus said. The Bible makes it clear, from Genesis to Revelation, that he alone will bring history to a conclusion. History will end when Jesus appears in majesty and glory.

Some claim that history is cyclical—it goes in cycles, and events often repeat themselves. In a limited sense, this is often true. But in a larger sense, we know that history is linear. It has a beginning, a middle, and an end.

The end of history has been planned and foretold.

The trajectory of history will come to a sudden halt.

The drama of history will reach a grand finale.

The pinnacle of history will be the glorious resurrection of believers.

The tragedy of history will be the judgment and dreadful end of unbelievers.

A LIFESTYLE OF GRATITUDE

Jesus is the Lord of history.

That is the message of the Bible, and it is especially the message of 1 and 2 Thessalonians. As we come to Paul's second epistle to the Thessalonians, we see that he is thrilled with the spiritual progress of this small group of believers in the coastal town of Thessalonica. They have been growing in the faith since he wrote his first epistle.

The Thessalonian believers do not have the kind of faith so often promoted by TV preachers—the "name-it-and-claim-it" teachings (or as I call it, "blab-it-and-grab-it"). That kind of populist theology treats God as a cosmic ATM machine—just insert your faith, punch in your prayer, and withdraw whatever you want.

According to this false doctrine, God wants you to have it all in the here and now. You have to feel sorry for the apostles and martyrs of the early church—if only they had had enough faith, they would have had gold chariots to ride around in, mansions in the ritziest section of Jerusalem, and vacation villas on the Sea of Galilee. Instead, most of them owned nothing, suffered persecution, and died by crucifixion, stoning, or beheading.

The Thessalonian believers understood that faith is not about getting it all in the here and now. The name-it-and-claim-it teachings so rampant today are nothing but self-worship falsely labeled as Christianity. One of the best antidotes to today's false doctrines is to take a realistic look at how first-century believers lived. The Christians in Thessalonica had no riches or luxuries to boast of, no magnificent, air-conditioned church building to worship in, no grand music programs for entertainment, and no radio or TV preachers to listen to. Their churches were not seeker-friendly.

For the Thessalonian believers, persecution was not something that happened to people on the other side of the world—it was their daily reality. Yet they didn't let the threats and attacks of the surrounding culture stop them from preaching the good news of Jesus Christ at every opportunity. They were bold and outspoken in their witness. They were mature in their faith. They believed that whether times were good or bad, whether they lived for Christ or died for Christ, Jesus would always be the Lord of history and the Lord of their circumstances.

So Paul takes up pen and parchment and composes his second letter to the church in Thessalonica. He begins with these words:

> Paul, Silas and Timothy,
>
> To the church of the Thessalonians in God our Father and the Lord Jesus Christ:
>
> Grace and peace to you from God the Father and the Lord Jesus Christ.
>
> We ought always to thank God for you, brothers and sisters, and rightly so, because your faith is growing more and more, and the love all of you have for one another is increasing. Therefore, among God's churches we boast about your perseverance and faith in all the persecutions and trials you are enduring (2 Thessalonians 1:1-4).

Paul opens with a greeting and a blessing of God's grace and peace upon the Thessalonian believers. Then he makes a remarkable statement, using a term that appears nowhere else in Scripture: "We ought always to thank God for you." The word translated "ought" means that he is bound or compelled or obligated to give thanks for the Thessalonian believers. He is saying that he stands in awe of their amazing endurance, love, and faith in the midst of troubled times. The focus of his grateful amazement is the intensity of their faith and mutual love: "your faith is growing more and more, and the love all of you have for one another is increasing."

Have you ever experienced gratitude like Paul's? Have you ever felt absolutely *compelled* by gratitude—so full of thanks that you couldn't hold it in? You might feel compelling gratitude when you or a loved one has a brush with death or when a frightening diagnosis turns out to be a false alarm. Our greatest experiences of gratitude usually accompany God's greatest gifts.

Sometimes the gifts of God's grace arrive amid the toughest of times. As the apostle James wrote, "Every good and perfect gift is from above, coming down from the Father of the heavenly lights, who does not change like shifting shadows" (James 1:17). Our circumstances may change for the worse, but God does not change. He delights in giving us gifts, often in the midst of our trials. It's only natural that we would want God to lift us out of our valley of trials and set us safely on a mountaintop. In a time of trial, God may give us a gift of endurance or spiritual insight or character growth, and we may not appreciate his gift at the time. When we are suffering, we don't want the gift of character growth—we just want the suffering to stop.

But sometimes, the greatest gift God gives us in our suffering is a Christlike spirit of acceptance. Sometimes, God actually gives us the supernatural grace to move beyond a natural human response, so that we can say, "Lord, thank you for what this trial is accomplishing in my life. I know that I am growing and learning and becoming sanctified in a way that I could never experience otherwise. Lord, I'm ready to cooperate with you as you transform this suffering into something good for my life and for your glory."

A few years ago, one of the leaders of our church went through a difficult medical challenge. After he recovered, he told me that he had a number of conversations with nonbelieving friends. When he told them that this crisis was the best thing that ever happened to him, they stared at him in amazement. They couldn't understand how he could be filled with gratitude to God while going through such a harrowing trial.

These are the growing-in-faith moments of life. These are the aha moments in our Christian walk. These experiences press us deeper into the arms of the Lord than any other life experience.

Paul lived a lifestyle of gratitude. Reflecting on the suffering and growth of the Thessalonian believers, his heart overflows with gratitude to God. The believers in Thessalonica had grown more Christlike through their suffering, and this realization sent Paul's heart leaping for joy.

G.K. Chesterton once wrote, "I would maintain that thanks are the highest form of thought; and that gratitude is happiness doubled by wonder."[26] And someone else once observed, "I pity the atheists. When they feel gratitude for life's blessings, they have no one to thank."

But Paul knows exactly who to thank for the faith and love of these steadfast believers in Thessalonica. The gratitude that burns in his heart is like a debt he owes to God. It is God who gives us the strength to trust him and love one another in tough times. God gives us power, not just to survive but to thrive in the lean times. God gives us the supernatural ability to persevere when it seems that all strength and hope are gone.

SUFFERING PRODUCES STRENGTH AND FAITH

The believers in Thessalonica were poor, oppressed, and persecuted. They were slandered and hated by their neighbors. And still their faith in God continued to grow. And when Paul learned of the growing faith of these beleaguered believers, he felt compelled to give thanks to God.

Many Christians today would have a hard time identifying with the faith of the Thessalonians. When we experience even a little bit of hardship, our faith comes crashing to earth. "I'm late for my hair appointment and I can't find my car keys! Lord, why me?" The believers in Thessalonica saw their livelihoods destroyed, their children attacked and beaten, and their homes vandalized because of their witness for Christ. They faced threats of arrest, imprisonment, and death. They were lied about and their reputations were destroyed. Through it all, their faith grew, and their love for one another intensified.

Instead of saying, "Why me?" they said, "Why not me? Why should I be treated any better than my Christian neighbors who are suffering?" Instead of saying, "Why are you doing this to me, Lord?" they said, "Thank you, Lord, for walking through this time of trial with me."

As you read these words, Christians around the world are undergoing incredible suffering for the sake of Christ. In many Muslim-dominated countries, where terrorism is a daily fact of life, Christians are being tortured and beheaded, and their children are murdered before their eyes. The Lord loves those martyred believers as much as he loves you and me.

The day may come when we will have to undergo persecution. Will our faith grow, as the faith of the Thessalonians grew? Will our love for one another intensify like the love of the Thessalonians? The time to start increasing our faith and deepening our Christlike character is now. We need to prepare ourselves now for the testing to come.

When Simon Peter was tested, he failed. Peter was a big talker, and he boasted repeatedly that even if all the other disciples abandoned Jesus, he would be faithful. So Jesus told Peter, "Simon, Simon, Satan has asked to sift all of you as wheat. But I have prayed for you, Simon, that your faith may not fail. And when you have turned back, strengthen your brothers."

Peter replied, "Lord, I am ready to go with you to prison and to death."

Then Jesus, his eyes full of sorrow, said, "I tell you, Peter, before the rooster crows today, you will deny three times that you know me" (see Luke 22:31-34).

It came to pass exactly as Jesus said. Peter's faith was shaken, and his failure would have surely destroyed him if Jesus hadn't prayed for him and given him a job to do: "When you have turned back, strengthen your brothers."

Jesus prayed for Simon Peter, and he prays for us today (Romans 8:34; Hebrews 7:25). Any strength we may have when we are going through trials and testing is due to this one fact: We have an Advocate in heaven. The same Advocate who interceded for Peter was interceding for the believers in Thessalonica, and he still intercedes for us today.

How can persecution be a source of strength instead of failure? How can persecution actually *increase* our faith instead of destroying it? Trials and sufferings drive us closer to the heart of God. Trials drive us to cling to God more tightly. Afflictions teach us to depend on God with every fiber of our being.

I have heard some religious teachers say, "We need to forgive God for allowing suffering in our lives. God means well, but he simply can't control all of life's contingencies. He can't help it. So we need to forgive him." That is nothing less than blasphemy. How dare any human being claim the right to "forgive" God?

God is good. God does only what is good. But what we *think* is good and what God *knows* is good are not always the same. That's why James, the brother of Jesus, said, "Consider it pure joy, my brothers and sisters, whenever you face trials of many kinds, because you know that the testing of your faith produces perseverance. Let perseverance finish its work so that you may be mature and complete, not lacking anything" (James 1:2-4).

We tend to speak of faith as if it were a tangible commodity that can be measured and weighed and quantified. People sometimes say, "I wish I had your faith," as if they were saying, "I wish I had your blue eyes," or "I wish I was as tall as you." Some people talk of faith as if it is here today, gone tomorrow—"I used to believe, but I lost my faith."

Faith is not something that can be weighed by the ounce. Faith is not something we inherit through our DNA. And faith is not something we can lose the way an absent-minded professor loses his glasses. Faith is a growing relationship of trust in the living God.

Relationships are dynamic, not static. Therefore, our trust relationship with God is equally dynamic. It's like a tree whose roots grow deeper into the soil and whose branches grow higher into the sky—but dies without water. It's like the muscles of an athlete—muscles that grow strong with exercise but atrophy when inactive.

If your faith is weak and spindly, you need to water it with the truth of God's Word. If your faith is flabby and atrophied, you need to exercise it by living in utter dependence on God. The believers in Thessalonica were continually in the Word as they tested and trusted God's promises.

Paul also gave thanks for the ever-intensifying love of the Thessalonian believers. Biblically mature Christians understand what authentic Christian love is. Christlike love is not gushy sentimentality. It's not a feeling or emotion. The love the Bible talks about, the love that is called *agape* in the Greek New Testament, is a decision, not a feeling.

Christlike love is a decision to embrace the unlovely, accept the unacceptable, forgive the unforgivable, and to bless when we feel like cursing. It's natural and easy to love people who are lovable. But God calls us to love even our enemies—and that kind of love is not natural. It's supernatural.

This supernatural, Christlike love is a decision to sacrifice our own interests for the sake of another person—even a person we don't like. It's the same kind of love Jesus had for us while we were lost in our sin. It's the same kind of love that led him to the cross to sacrifice himself for our sake.

Many people think that, when faced with an unlovable person, they need to grit their teeth and try to love that person in their own strength. You can't do that. Christlike love can come only from Christ himself.

Faith tends to grow organically, gradually, over time, like a tree. But love can overflow like a river, flooding and saturating our lives. When the love of Christ floods your life, he fills you with a supernatural love that overflows to others. He loves people through you. You can't help yourself. When your life is filled with his love, you are simply carried along by the flood.

The best and strongest marriages are made up of three kinds of love—what the Greeks called *eros* (romantic love), *phileo* (friendship love), and *agape* (Christlike love). When a husband and wife truly love each other in all three of these ways, they are practically tripping over each other to serve each other, sacrifice for each other, give to each other, and forgive each other. If the love of Christ dies in their relationship— if they stop living out *agape* love toward one another—then they stop serving each other and forgiving each other. Soon they start nitpicking each other's little mistakes and sins. What was once a flood of the love of Christ in their lives has dried up and become a parched desert.

But their love, their relationship, their marriage doesn't have to end that way. If a husband and wife will turn back to Christ and love each other as he loved them, as he commands them, their *agape* love will come flooding back. And when the *agape* love floods back into their lives, the *eros* and *phileo* will return as well.

There's an analogy here to Paul's love for the Thessalonian believers. He was well aware of their flaws and shortcomings. He knew they were not perfect people. But like that newly married husband and wife, in the throes of an intense young love, Paul overlooked their faults and failings. The love of Christ so overwhelmed his heart that he focused on the great transforming change God had brought into the Thessalonian church. And he thanked God for their ever-increasing faith and their ever-intensifying love.

GODLY BOASTING

Paul's primary concern for the Thessalonians was that the intense afflictions they experienced might cause them to lose hope. But Timothy reported the good news that, far from losing hope, they were standing firm in the hope of their eternal salvation. To them, the storms of life were like water splashing against the immovable Rock of their hope in Christ. The believers could not be moved or shaken.

As a result of this report, Paul was filled with a righteous and godly pride for them. He wrote, "Therefore, among God's churches we boast about your perseverance and faith in all the persecutions and trials you are enduring." Paul boasted! There is nothing wrong with Paul's godly pride and his boasting about the perseverance and faith of the Thessalonian believers. This kind of boasting is perfectly compatible with Christian humility. Was Paul taking credit for the perseverance and faith of the Thessalonians? No! Paul gives all the glory to God.

Paul is boasting about what God has done in the lives of these believers. He is proud of the grace and power and love of God. His boasting in the Lord is simply the flip side of his gratitude to the Lord.

In the mid-1970s, I spent five years serving several congregations in Australia. I can count on one hand the number of times anyone came up to me and said, "Thank you for preaching the Word," or "Thank you for staying true to the Scriptures." Why didn't anyone say that to me? Because they feared it might go to my head. They were afraid that compliments might make me prideful. That's part of the Australian culture.

Here in America, people tend to be more effusive. They feel freer to praise and thank the pastor. To be candid, I think the Australian way might be the better way. Perhaps in a desire to show appreciation to the pastor and help the pastor feel loved and affirmed, we might be leading some down the path toward unhealthy pride.

So what does the Bible teach? If we look closely at the Scriptures, we see that neither effusive flattery nor a stony silence is biblical. While flattery produces unhealthy pride, withholding thanks and appreciation can produce discouragement. Paul shows us that we can affirm people without tempting them to be prideful. Notice how Paul affirms the Thessalonian Christians.

He says, in effect, "I thank God for you. I thank God for giving you his gifts. I thank God for giving you his strength. I thank God for giving you such faith. I thank God for doing this great work in you." When Paul affirms the Thessalonian believers, he gives glory to God, not to the believers themselves. Yes, he affirms their character growth and faith and mutual love—but he gives all the credit to God.

Why is that important? Because history is coming to an end and we need to be faithful to God. We need to love one another. We need to hold fast to our hope in him. We need to lift one another up.

As we will see in the rest of 2 Thessalonians, the signs of the Lord's return are all around us. He could come at any moment. In the rest of this book, we'll talk about how to be prepared for his return.

10

HOW TO DESTROY YOUR ENEMIES

2 Thessalonians 1:5-12

D uring the Civil War, President Abraham Lincoln spoke at an official White House reception, saying that the Confederates should be viewed not as enemies to be exterminated but as fellow human beings with mistaken views about slavery. One woman who attended the reception was outraged at Lincoln's plea that the Confederates be forgiven. She confronted him and demanded to know how he could possibly speak kindly of his enemies instead of demanding their destruction.

"Why, madam," Lincoln said, "do I not destroy my enemies when I make them my friends?"[27]

That was Lincoln's overriding philosophy from his early years to the end of his life. He always believed it was wiser to seek reconciliation instead of revenge, compassion instead of condemnation. As a young lawyer in Illinois, he did something few attorneys would do today: He encouraged prospective clients *not* to go to court but to reach an out-of-court compromise. He passed up a lot of fees that way, but he believed he made the world a better place.

Lincoln once gave a lecture to a group of attorneys, saying, "Discourage litigation. Persuade your neighbors to compromise whenever you can. Point out to them how the nominal winner is often a real loser—in fees, expenses, and waste of time. As a peacemaker the lawyer has a superior opportunity of being a good man. There will still be business enough."[28]

On one occasion, a man came to Lincoln eager for revenge against a debtor. The debtor owed this man two dollars and fifty cents but had no way to pay him. Lincoln tried to persuade the man to drop the matter and forgive the debt, reminding him that his legal fee would be ten dollars. Did he really want to spend ten dollars in a futile effort to collect two dollars and fifty cents? The client insisted on getting his revenge.

So Lincoln collected the ten dollars as a retainer. Then he went to the debtor and gave him five dollars. The debtor then paid the plaintiff two dollars and fifty cents—and pocketed the rest. The plaintiff, happy to get the money he was owed, apparently never found out that he'd been repaid with his own money. Though he had incurred a net loss of seven dollars and fifty cents, and the defendant was two dollars and fifty cents richer, the plaintiff felt he had gotten his revenge—and amazingly, he was *satisfied* with the outcome.[29]

The hunger for revenge can drive people to foolish extremes. In nineteenth-century England, a woman went to her minister for counseling. Her husband had been treating her badly, and she had tried to be patient with him, but she was at the end of her rope. She asked her pastor what she should do.

Her pastor suggested she "heap burning coals on his head." He was referring, of course, to Proverbs 25:21-22, where Solomon says that if we treat an enemy with kindness, we will "heap burning coals on his head." Unfortunately, this woman was not familiar with the biblical metaphor.

When she returned the following week, the minister asked her, "So, did you take my advice? Did you 'heap burning coals on his head'?"

"No, Pastor," she replied. "I thought of putting fire on my husband's head, but I decided instead to try boiling water."[30]

I hope I'm leaving no room for misunderstanding—God intends that the "burning coals" you heap on your enemy are acts of kindness, not acts of revenge. They are intended to burn the conscience, not the flesh.

LIFE IS UNFAIR—BUT JUSTICE IS COMING

Human nature dictates that when someone hurts us, we avenge the wrong, that we pay our enemy back double or triple the injury he dealt us. But God tells us we are to love our enemies and bless those who persecute us.

Our enemies are a valuable spiritual asset. Critics and false accusers can help keep us spiritually strong. A pastor friend of mine in Southern California used to say, "Rejoice when they kick you in the backside. That means you're out in front!"

Another benefit of having enemies is that they keep us on our knees in prayer. When attacked, most of us think to pray for ourselves and our wounded feelings. If we are specially attuned to the will of God, we will also be on our knees, praying for those who have hurt us. That's the response Paul saw in the Thessalonian believers to the persecution they suffered.

The Thessalonians didn't seek revenge against their persecutors. They blessed their persecutors and demonstrated increasing signs of spiritual maturity. They were looking forward to the day when Christ would appear and bring history to conclusion. In the meantime, they were living peaceable lives, paying back evil with good, and advancing the gospel in the midst of persecution.

Paul does not suggest that those who are persecuting the church should not be held accountable for their actions. In fact, Paul assured the Thessalonians that God himself would punish the evildoers:

> All this is evidence that God's judgment is right, and as a result you will be counted worthy of the kingdom of God, for which you are suffering. God is just: He will pay back trouble to those who trouble you and give relief to you who are troubled, and to us as well. This will happen when the Lord Jesus is revealed from heaven in blazing fire with his powerful angels. He will punish those who do not know God and do not obey the gospel of our Lord Jesus. They will be punished with everlasting destruction and shut out from the presence of the Lord and from the glory of his might

on the day he comes to be glorified in his holy people and
to be marveled at among all those who have believed. This
includes you, because you believed our testimony to you
(2 Thessalonians 1:5-10).

Paul reminds the Thessalonians that God is just, and he will repay
those who have done evil toward God's people. When will God's vengeance be unleashed? "This will happen when the Lord Jesus is revealed
from heaven in blazing fire with his powerful angels," Paul says.

The Bible never pretends that evil isn't real. The Bible never min-
imizes pain, suffering, or sin, but calls each by its rightful name. The
Bible never pretends that you will always be rewarded if you do good.
Life is unfair, and our good deeds are often punished, not rewarded.
But the Bible also tells us that when believers suffer unjustly, when we
are baptized by fire, God is with us in a special way and sustains us
through times of unjust suffering.

In the final analysis, God does not overlook injustice. He does not
let evildoers off scot-free. He does not let false accusers get away with
their crimes. Suffering and persecution can produce Christlike character within us—but that does not give others the right to do evil toward
us. "God is just," Paul says. "He will pay back trouble to those who
trouble you and give relief to you who are troubled."

Today, believers are ridiculed, rejected, and killed for their faith.
At the Lord's return, they will be richly rewarded. Today, unbelievers
seem to profit from their sin. At the Lord's return, they will be punished, plunged into an eternity of suffering and regret.

When Jesus the Judge appears, everything you see today will be
turned upside down. Those who call good "evil" and evil "good" will
finally be forced to acknowledge that only God is good—and they
themselves have done evil. They will not escape the consequences of
their rejection of God and their mistreatment of God's people.

In this passage, Paul answers three questions that trouble the beleaguered Christians of Thessalonica:

1. When will God vindicate believers and judge nonbelievers?

2. Who will be punished?

3. What form will that punishment take?

Let's examine each of those questions in turn.

QUESTION 1: WHEN WILL GOD VINDICATE AND AVENGE HIS PEOPLE?

As we've seen, the return of Jesus Christ will be the climax of history. His appearance will bring to an end all opportunities for repentance and salvation. His return will be a moment that divides the world into two distinct groups—the saved and the unsaved, the just and the unjust, those whose names are written in the Book of Life and those who have no part in Christ. Jesus himself described that moment this way:

> "When the Son of Man comes in his glory, and all the angels with him, he will sit on his glorious throne. All the nations will be gathered before him, and he will separate the people one from another as a shepherd separates the sheep from the goats. He will put the sheep on his right and the goats on his left" (Matthew 25:31-33).

The world will be divided between sheep and goats—and many who think they are sheep will discover to their everlasting dismay that they are goats and that Jesus, the good shepherd, never knew them.

At the return of Christ, the world will be turned upside down, and everything that is lifted up in pride will be cast down, and everything that is held down by oppression and humiliation will be raised up. In the here and now, the glory of Jesus is hidden. In the here and now, the Lord's followers are oppressed and persecuted. In the here and now, the name of Jesus is used as a swear word.

But when the moment of the Lord's glorious appearing strikes like lightning and he splits the eastern sky, he will be revealed to believers and unbelievers alike. It will be the moment that the Greek New Testament calls the *apokalypsis*, from which we get our English word *apocalypse*. In the Greek, this word literally means a revelation or an unveiling or an uncovering.

Today, the righteous power of the Lord Jesus Christ is hidden from the world—but in that day it will be fully revealed. Today his absolute wisdom and justice are ignored and mocked—but in that day his righteousness will tower over a terrified world. Today, arrogant men strut around as if they are gods—but in that day they will beg the rocks to fall on them and hide them from the Lord's face. Today, many churches and church leaders deny that Jesus is God—but in that day they will fall on their faces before him.

When Jesus first came to earth two thousand years ago, he came in humility as a helpless baby. When he returns, he will come in glory as the King of all creation, wielding an iron scepter. And he will not return alone. Paul tells us in 2 Thessalonians 1:7, "This will happen when the Lord Jesus is revealed from heaven in blazing fire with his powerful angels." He will appear in a blazing fire, accompanied by his mighty angels. Where did Paul learn this? From Jesus himself: "For the Son of Man is going to come in his Father's glory with his angels, and then he will reward each person according to what they have done" (Matthew 16:27).

What does Paul mean when he says that the Lord will return in "blazing fire"? This is the fire of God's judgment, the intense inferno of his justice, the white-hot furnace that destroys and consumes God's enemies. With this "blazing fire," God will avenge his faithful children.

This fire reveals God's twofold justice. It means relief to all believers—and retribution to all unbelievers. It means peace and rest to all believers—and pain and suffering to all enemies of the Lord. This fire, the natural sun-like brilliance of God's glory, holds no terrors for those who belong to the Lord. But for unbelievers and evildoers, there will be no escape. With this fire, God will vindicate his people and destroy those who persecuted his people.

QUESTION 2: WHO WILL RECEIVE RETRIBUTION AND PUNISHMENT?

Those who have denied Jesus as their Savior, those who have rejected him as the only way to heaven, those who have mocked and persecuted his children will receive retribution and punishment on the day that he returns. Paul wrote in verses 8 and 9, "He will punish those who do not know God and do not obey the gospel of our Lord Jesus. They will be punished with everlasting destruction and shut out from the presence of the Lord and from the glory of his might."

God's punishment will not be an act of out-of-control anger or hatred. The punishment he metes out will represent God's perfect wisdom and flawless understanding of human beings and the evil they do. No one will protest, "Your verdict is unjust! I'm innocent! The sentence is too harsh! You have judged me unfairly!" No, God's judgment is flawless. The punishment will fit the crime. All who are sentenced will be without excuse.

That's why Paul wrote, "Do not take revenge, my dear friends, but leave room for God's wrath, for it is written: 'It is mine to avenge; I will repay,' says the Lord" (Romans 12:19). Human justice is flawed because it is based on limited understanding. But God's justice is flawless, perfect, and complete because it is based on the limitless wisdom of God.

John the Baptist spoke of the justice of God in thundering terms: "His winnowing fork is in his hand, and he will clear his threshing floor, gathering his wheat into the barn and burning up the chaff with unquenchable fire" (Matthew 3:12). So much for the milquetoast stereotype of Jesus—the "gentle Jesus, meek and mild." Yes, Jesus is the sacrificial Lamb of God. Yes, he blesses the children, heals the sick, mends the broken-hearted, and forgives and restores sinners—today. But when he returns, he will not come as a lamb. He will come with blazing fire to judge the world.

Those who preach only the mercy of Jesus—who deliberately or ignorantly omit his justice—are preaching a *false* gospel. Jesus himself said that the day of his return would be "the time of punishment in fulfillment of all that has been written" (Luke 21:22). Many churchgoers today don't want to hear that message. Many pastors today don't want to preach that message. They wish they could cut those sections out of the Bible.

But we dare not alter God's Word to suit our preferences. God warned Israel, "Do not add to what I command you and do not subtract from it, but keep the commands of the LORD your God that I give you" (Deuteronomy 4:2).

And Proverbs 30:5-6 tells us,

> Every word of God is flawless;
>   he is a shield to those who take refuge in him.
> Do not add to his words,
>   or he will rebuke you and prove you a liar.

And Jesus, speaking through the apostle John, says, "I warn everyone who hears the words of the prophecy of this scroll: If anyone adds anything to them, God will add to that person the plagues described in this scroll. And if anyone takes words away from this scroll of prophecy, God will take away from that person any share in the tree of life and in the Holy City, which are described in this scroll" (Revelation 22:18).

We must hear and preach the full counsel of God's Word, no more, no less.

The Word of God tells us that the return of the Lord Jesus will be a day of vengeance, a day of vindication, a day of exacting and fitting punishment, a day of carefully measured judgment, and a day of perfect righteousness. Jesus, the most perfect of all judges, will be flawless in judgment.

Who will be punished? Those who have refused to believe that Jesus alone is the way, the truth, and the life. This will be an enormous human tragedy—but a tragedy the unbelievers have brought on themselves. They will have no one else to blame—least of all Jesus, the righteous Judge. Those who bring this tragedy upon themselves will include the outright enemies of God, the atheists and secularists who have mocked God and persecuted his people.

But it will also include, I fear, many who label themselves "Christians" or "evangelicals," but who openly deny, and teach others to deny, that Jesus is the only way to God the Father. They've tried to have it both ways, claiming to be teachers of God's Word while seeking friendship with the world. As the Scriptures remind us, "Anyone who chooses to be a friend of the world becomes an enemy of God" (James 4:4).

And all who are enemies of God will face judgment when the Lord returns.

QUESTION 3: WHAT FORM
WILL THAT PUNISHMENT TAKE?

What form will God's punishment of his enemies take? Paul answers: "They will be punished with everlasting destruction and shut out from the presence of the Lord and from the glory of his might on the day he comes to be glorified in his holy people and to be marveled at among all those who have believed" (1:9-10).

The word *destruction* does not mean "annihilation." It does not mean God's enemies will be vaporized. The Scriptures tell us that they will wish they could simply disappear—but that option will not be available to them. The destruction they will suffer means they will lose everything that makes existence worthwhile. They will be left empty and without hope. They will pay for their rejection of the Lord Jesus Christ throughout eternity, even as the Lord's followers will be blessed and rewarded throughout eternity.

The Lord's enemies—all those who rejected Christ and refused to place their trust in him—will be consigned to a place of "everlasting destruction." Annihilation would be instantaneous destruction— it would take place in a matter of seconds or even milliseconds, and then it would be over. Those who are annihilated would cease to exist. But "everlasting destruction" speaks of a form of destruction that goes on and on, without end, without relief.

Paul adds that those who are destroyed will be "shut out from the presence of the Lord and from the glory of his might." The image here is of God's enemies completely separated from the Lord, yet fully aware—moment by moment and age by age—that they are forever shut out and denied a place in heaven with the Lord. There is no hint or suggestion of instantaneous annihilation, only everlasting despair for those who reject Christ.

Paul also says that when the Lord returns, he will be "glorified in his holy people" and all believers will marvel at him. "This includes you," Paul adds, "because you believed our testimony to you." Else-where, Paul tells us that we will have bodies like the glorified resurrec-tion body of the Lord Jesus (see Philippians 3:21). Not only will our bodies be Christlike, but our character will be Christlike. He will be glorified in us, and we will be glorified in him.

God has promised you and me, as followers of Christ, an expe-rience of glory so amazing that it will take our breath away. We will hardly be able to express our amazement. Paul then adds:

> With this in mind, we constantly pray for you, that our God may make you worthy of his calling, and that by his power he may bring to fruition your every desire for goodness and your every deed prompted by faith. We pray this so that the name of our Lord Jesus may be glorified in you, and you in him, according to the grace of our God and the Lord Jesus Christ (2 Thessalonians 1:11-12).

Paul prays for the Thessalonian believers that they will always be encouraged, empowered, and motivated by the hope of that coming day. We must always pray for one another that we will look forward to that day as we labor joyfully for him. Instead of spending our lives filled with fear of terrorism, anger over government corruption, bitter-ness over unfair attacks from our enemies, woundedness over betray-als by our friends, we should pray for one another and encourage one another to be ready for the Lord's return.

Jesus is preparing an amazing eternal home for us where—and this is grace beyond our comprehension!—*we will actually reign with him.* Paul prays that the Lord Jesus will be glorified through our lives in the here and now so that we may one day be glorified through him in eternity.

HOW WILL YOU DESTROY YOUR ENEMY?

In April 1942, American bombardier Jake DeShazer crouched in the belly of a B-25 bomber. His plane flew low over the Japanese coast-line, barely clearing the treetops on its way to Tokyo. Nearing the target,

DeShazer released the bombs, destroying a fuel storage facility and delivering America's reply to the attack on Pearl Harbor four months earlier.

As the bomber flew west toward China, exploding flak punched holes in the bomber's skin. Hours later, the engines sputtered and died—and Jake and his fellow airmen bailed out over China.

What Jake DeShazer didn't know then, and wouldn't learn until months later, was that at about the same time he was jumping out of his doomed plane, his mother was awakened in the middle of the night in far-off America. She didn't even know that her son was flying a mission over Japan, yet she felt an intense burden to pray for her son. Jake had been raised by Christian parents, yet he had never received Jesus as Lord and Savior.

As this young man fell through the skies over Japanese-occupied China, he didn't think to pray. He didn't think about God at all.

DeShazer landed hard in a graveyard, breaking several ribs. Minutes later, he was surrounded by Japanese soldiers who knew he had taken part in the raid on Tokyo. Thus began his four-year ordeal as prisoner of war. DeShazer lived in a tiny cell, which he left only when being questioned or tortured. Sometimes his captors beat him or hung him by his hands for hours. He spent most of those four years sick with dysentery and other illnesses.

Two years into his imprisonment, DeShazer's captors permitted him to have a Bible for three weeks. He read it by the light of a tiny slit near the top of his prison cell. He read the Bible from cover to cover. By the time he had to give the Bible back, he had memorized many long passages—and he had committed his life to Christ.

Soon after he became a Christian, Jake DeShazer underwent a test of his commitment to follow Christ. One of his guards was a sadistic man who delighted in torturing the American prisoners. He slammed a cell door on DeShazer's foot—and DeShazer felt an immediate impulse to swear at the man. But before he could voice his anger, he felt the Lord's voice speaking to him from the Sermon on the Mount: "Love your enemies and pray for those who persecute you" (Matthew 5:44). The following day, DeShazer blessed the guard in Japanese and asked about his family. The amazed guard brought him an extra ration of food that evening.

After the war, Jake DeShazer returned to the United States, married, and attended seminary. He and his wife later returned to Japan as missionaries. They lived among the Japanese people for three decades, and led many to Christ. In one of those ironies that only God can engineer, one of DeShazer's converts was Mitsuo Fuchida—a former captain in the Imperial Japanese Navy Air Service and the man who had led the attack on Pearl Harbor.

Through Jake DeShazer's witness, God led Mitsuo Fuchida to become an evangelist. Fuchida traveled throughout Japan and all around the world, preaching to vast crowds. Because Jake DeShazer gave up the right to revenge, choosing instead to love his enemies and pray for his persecutors, God used him to reach many Japanese people for Christ. And God used one of DeShazer's converts, the leader of the attack on Pearl Harbor, to reach thousands more.

"Do I not destroy my enemies," Lincoln said, "when I make them my friends?" This is a principle that comes straight from the words of Jesus, a principle that Jake DeShazer came to understand very well and put into practice in a powerful way. When Mitsuo Fuchida gave his heart to the Lord Jesus Christ, Jake DeShazer's "revenge" was complete. He had "destroyed" his enemy by making him a brother in Christ and a fellow evangelist.

Who is the enemy in your life that you would like to "destroy"? How will you "destroy" your enemy with love, kindness, and the good news of Jesus Christ?

11

THE BIG DANGER
OF SMALL FLAWS

2 Thessalonians 2:1-5

D on Shula was head coach of the Baltimore Colts from 1963
to 1969 and head coach of the Miami Dolphins from 1970 to
1995. He coached the Dolphins to two Super Bowl victories
and the only perfect season in the history of the NFL. He had only two
losing seasons in his thirty-six years as an NFL head coach.

In 1984, the *New York Times* published a profile of Coach Don
Shula that revealed one of the secrets—perhaps the most *important*
secret—of his coaching success. The key to the "Shula System," the
Times observed, is "the coach's search for perfection in practice." Coach
Shula himself explained: "We never let an error go unchallenged.
Uncorrected errors will multiply."

When the reporter asked if it might not be a good idea to occasionally overlook a small flaw in practice, Coach Shula replied with a question: "What is a small flaw?"[31]

This is a question we should all ask ourselves daily, even hourly.
What is a small flaw in my integrity, in my morality, in my honesty, in
my relationship with God? And what is a small flaw in a church, in its
doctrines, in the way that church teaches God's truth, in the way the
congregation lives out God's commands?

On January 28, 1986, the space shuttle *Challenger* was destroyed in
an explosion seventy-three seconds after liftoff. Seven crew members

perished, and the space shuttle program was shut down for almost three years. The cause of the explosion? A rubber O-ring seal in the shuttle's right solid rocket booster. The O-ring became brittle in the icy January weather, and it cracked, permitting hot gases to escape. Those flaming gases burned through the skin of the external fuel tank, exploding the shuttle.

What is a small flaw? A small flaw is a tiny crack in a rubber O-ring—and it was the difference between life and death for seven people.

On February 1, 2003, the space shuttle *Columbia* was reentering the earth's atmosphere, headed toward a scheduled landing in California, when it broke apart, its pieces streaking across the sky like a swarm of meteors. Once again, seven crew members perished, and the space shuttle program was shut down for more than two years. NASA engineers found that a small piece of insulating foam had broken off the external fuel tank during liftoff, striking the left wing of the shuttle, damaging one of the heat-shield tiles. As the shuttle descended during its final approach, the broken tile allowed superheated atmospheric gases to penetrate the wing and break the ship apart.

What is a small flaw? A small flaw is a piece of plastic foam that cracks a heat-shield tile during launch—and it was the difference between life and death for seven people.

Every disaster starts with a small flaw. A raging forest fire can start from a tiny spark. The fatal car crash can result from a split-second of inattention. And a seemingly minor deviation from God's truth can lead a believer into a catastrophic heresy.

As we come to the second chapter of Paul's second letter to the Thessalonians, we see that there are huge spiritual dangers hidden within the smallest flaws in our thinking. When it comes to God's truth, there is no such thing as a small flaw. There is no such thing as a harmless error.

YOUR SPIRITUAL O-RING

In America, and throughout Western civilization, we pride ourselves on our tolerant and pluralistic culture. While it is good to tolerate people who are different from us, we must remember that not all ideas and beliefs are equal. The fact that we seek to live in peace with people of other faiths does not mean we believe all religions are equally true, nor do we believe that all religions lead to the same God.

God's message to Israel, delivered through Moses, is the same message God has for us today: "I AM WHO I AM" (Exodus 3:14). God has never said, "I am whatever you want me to be." He has never said, "I am whoever you believe I am." Yet this error persists in all times, in all cultures, and is even taught in many churches today. Jesus and all the apostles battled this heresy throughout the New Testament.

What's wrong with the notion that the God of the Bible, the God of Abraham, Isaac, and Jacob, is also the God of the Mormons and Jehovah's Witnesses, the "All-Glorious" of the Baha'i, Krishna of the Hindus, Allah of the Muslims, and on and on? Isn't it possible that all these religions simply grope toward the same God but under different names?

It sounds like such a reasonable question: Maybe these other religions are just a little bit flawed in their understanding. Does that mean there's nothing we can learn from other religions? Does that mean we should have nothing to do with other religions and the people who believe them?

The truth is that there truly is nothing we can learn from other religions. Darkness has nothing to teach the light. Mohammed has nothing to teach Jesus. That doesn't mean we have nothing to do with people of other religions. We can be kind. We can love them with the love of Jesus. We can witness to them. We can evangelize them. In fact, we can learn enough about their religion that we can witness to them even more effectively.

But we should always remember that other religions are designed to deceive people and lead them into darkness. Don't fall for their deception. Don't let the spiritual darkness of other religions overshadow you. The moment you start to question the truth of the Bible, the moment you begin to forget the truth that opened your eyes and saved you, you have opened yourself to that small spiritual flaw.

You have allowed a tiny crack in your spiritual O-ring.

You have permitted a tiny breach in the tiles of your spiritual heat-shield.

What is a small flaw? What harm could it do? That's the question Paul confronted as he wrote the second letter to the church in Thessalonica. In the first chapter, Paul thanked God for the persevering faith of the Thessalonian believers in the midst of trials and persecution. But all was not well with the believers in Thessalonica. False teachers had come into the church, and they preached a deceptive "gospel."

These false teachers were wicked to the point of forgery. They had evidently produced a spurious letter supposedly from the apostle Paul. This false letter stated that the Lord's return had already occurred. So you can imagine the anxiety and even panic that these believers felt. Here they had been living faithfully for the Lord, expecting his return at any time. They were increasing daily in faith and good works. They were growing daily in love for one another. Their hope for Christ's return was intensifying.

But false teachers had infiltrated the church, spreading lies and shaking the confidence of the Thessalonian believers. So Paul picked up his pen and exposed the lies of the false teachers and expounded the truth about the second coming of Christ:

> Concerning the coming of our Lord Jesus Christ and our being gathered to him, we ask you, brothers and sisters, not to become easily unsettled or alarmed by the teaching allegedly from us—whether by a prophecy or by word of mouth or by letter—asserting that the day of the Lord has already come. Don't let anyone deceive you in any way, for that day will not come until the rebellion occurs and the man of lawlessness is revealed, the man doomed to destruction. He will oppose and will exalt himself over everything that is called God or is worshiped, so that he sets himself up in God's temple, proclaiming himself to be God.

> Don't you remember that when I was with you I used to tell you these things? (2 Thessalonians 2:1-5).

Paul wanted to alleviate the fears the false teachers had stirred up. In this passage, he gives us details about the Lord's return that are not found anywhere else in Scripture. Paul's account is consistent with other prophetic passages, but much more detailed. In his first letter to the Thessalonians, Paul had assured the believers that the rapture, the *Parousia*, had not yet taken place.

When we are going through crushing circumstances, our minds can wreak havoc on us. Our imaginations can go wild and our hearts can come unglued. It is easy to doubt in the darkness all the truths we so confidently accepted in the daylight. Satan uses these opportunities to attack our faith and paralyze us. As long as we are locked in a strait-jacket of doubt, Satan has us defeated. He cannot steal our salvation from us, but he can render us ineffective in our service to God.

ENTER THE ANTICHRIST

The Thessalonian believers were so shaken by their crushing circumstances that the lies of the false teachers began to make terrifying sense. What if it were true? What if the Lord's return had already taken place—and these believers in Thessalonica had been left behind?

Paul countered these lies with the truth about the events that must take place before the Lord's return: "that day will not come until the rebellion occurs and the man of lawlessness is revealed, the man doomed to destruction."

The original Greek term that the NIV translates "the rebellion" is often rendered as "the apostasy" or "the falling away." This refers to a great global rejection of God's truth, particularly by people who are in the church. We already see increasing signs in the church today that many who claim to be Christians or evangelicals are denying the truth of God's Word and denying that Jesus is the way, the truth, and the life.

The Thessalonian believers knew what Paul meant when he referred to "the man of lawlessness." Most of them were Jewish Christians, converted by Paul's preaching in the synagogue at Thessalonica (see Acts 17:1-4). So they were well acquainted with the Hebrew Scriptures, including Daniel 9:20-27, which contains the angel Gabriel's prophecy of the antichrist. It's the same passage Jesus referred to in his Olivet Discourse: "So when you see standing in the holy place 'the abomination that causes desolation,' spoken of through the prophet Daniel...then there will be great distress, unequaled from the beginning of the world until now—and never to be equaled again" (Matthew 24:15,21).

Here is the biblical truth: There have always been evil leaders in the world. There were wicked tyrants ruling Rome in the first century. There are wicked tyrants ruling many nations in the twenty-first century. Think of the worst dictators of the past century—Hitler, Mussolini, Stalin, Mao. Then consider this: When the long-prophesied antichrist is revealed, he will surpass them all. The antichrist is known throughout Scripture by many different names. Paul calls him "the man of lawlessness," "the lawless one," and "the man doomed to destruction." John, in the book of Revelation, refers to him as "the beast."

The antichrist is the one whose activities are in accordance with the will of Satan. The apostle John named him the antichrist because he is against Christ, opposed to Christ, the usurper of Christ's place, and the opposite of all that Christ is. John says there are many antichrists in the world—false teachers who spread a false gospel. But in 1 John 2:18, John tells us that, in addition to the many false teachers and antichrists, there is one *specific* antichrist, *one man* who will one day dominate the world scene.

Anyone who opposes the person of Christ, the work of Christ, the divinity of Christ, the uniqueness of Christ, and the truth of Christ has manifested the spirit of antichrist. But the final antichrist, Satan's ultimate creation, will combine all the worst characteristics of all the antichrists and false teachers throughout human history.

Ever since Satan tempted Adam and Eve in the Garden of Eden, he has been trying to thwart God's plan of salvation. Every time Satan tries to derail God's plan, he fails miserably—yet he leaves a trail of death, grief, and destruction in his wake.

Satan tried to murder the Messiah in the cradle by influencing King Herod to slay all the male children under two years old, but Joseph and Mary took Jesus to safety in Egypt (see Matthew 2). When Jesus presented himself as the Messiah in Nazareth, Satan inspired the crowd to drive him out of town and throw him off a cliff, but Jesus eluded their grasp (see Luke 4). Satan even tried to deflect Jesus from his mission, using Peter, the chief disciple, to urge Jesus not to go to the cross, but Jesus recognized the true instigator behind Peter's words and said, "Get behind me, Satan!" (Matthew 16:23).

When Jesus died on the cross, Satan might have thought he had won a victory over Jesus. Perhaps Satan even hoped he had thwarted God's plan by torturing and murdering the long-prophesied Messiah. But on the third day, Jesus rose victorious over the grave—and destroyed Satan's hope of overturning God's plan.

Ever since that time, century after century, Satan has tried to overthrow the work of God by unleashing irrational hatred against the followers of Jesus. His last desperate stratagem will be a demon-possessed man, a political and religious leader of absolute evil who will serve as Satan's instrument—a human puppet to do his bidding—the antichrist.

DANIEL'S VISION OF THE ANTICHRIST

Daniel symbolically pictured the antichrist as a "little horn" that arose from a vicious ten-horned beast. This "little horn" will rise from obscurity to a place of global prominence. He will be a man of great intelligence, an articulate and persuasive speaker, and an influential global leader like no other leader in human history. He will change the laws and the times and the seasons, replacing ancient religious observances into ceremonies and celebrations that honor him alone. He will introduce an immoral and satanic "morality" that will drag the human race even deeper into the muck of sin and self-defilement than it already is today.

Daniel 8:23 describes this satanic leader as "a fierce-looking king, a master of intrigue," meaning that he will threaten, intimidate, and manipulate people into submission. He will be skilled in the art of political intrigue. He will weaponize language and doubletalk so skillfully as to make George Orwell's "Big Brother" seem amateurish by comparison. His intellect, his political skills, his manipulative craft will all be derived directly from Satan himself. Daniel 7:26 tells us that this antichrist will be unstoppable by any human means. Only God can destroy him.

And God *will* destroy him.

The antichrist will first appear as a benefactor to the world, and especially to Israel. He will seem sympathetic to all nations and ethnic groups, and they will be eager to give him their allegiance. To the Christians—especially those who are undiscerning—he will be a Christian. To the Jews, he will be as one of them. To the Muslims, he will be as one of them. To the atheists and agnostics, he will seem to be as enlightened, worldly, and secular as they think themselves to be.

The antichrist will make a seven-year covenant with Israel, and then midway through the term of that covenant, he will reveal his true intentions as the angel Gabriel explains in Daniel's prophecy:

> "He will confirm a covenant with many for one 'seven.' In the middle of the 'seven' he will put an end to sacrifice and offering. And at the temple he will set up an abomination that causes desolation, until the end that is decreed is poured out on him" (Daniel 9:27).

The antichrist will defile the temple in Jerusalem with an "abomination that causes desolation." Paul himself describes the "abomination" this way: "He will oppose and will exalt himself over everything that is called God or is worshiped, so that he sets himself up in God's temple, proclaiming himself to be God" (2:4). Praise be to God, the antichrist's reign of terror will be short-lived—but while it lasts, it will be murderous and horrifying beyond our imagining.

Finally, as we see in Revelation 19:20, the Lord will destroy the antichrist and his evil kingdom. That's why Paul encourages the Thessalonian believers not to panic, not to "become easily unsettled or alarmed." Unlike so many end-times preachers (both the first-century variety and the twenty-first-century variety), Paul is not peddling sensationalism. He is not trying to get rich by playing on the fear and curiosity of his readers

Paul desired only to comfort the believers, not confuse them. He sought to encourage the believers, not unsettle them. He longed to correct the errors the false teachers had inflicted on them and to restore the joy the false teachers had stolen from them.

"Don't let anyone deceive you in any way," he said. Why was this so important to Paul? Why was he so intensely concerned that they not be misled? It's because false ideas easily lead to anxiety and fear. False ideas can lead a person to abandon the truth. False ideas can lead a person to become disheartened and discouraged. Paul loves the Thessalonian believers—they are his spiritual children. He led them to the Lord, so he has a special affection for them. He does not want to see them fall prey to false teaching and the anxiety, fear, and discouragement it brings.

Unfortunately, deception is all too commonplace in the church of Jesus Christ today. Satan disguises himself as an angel of light, a bearer of truth. False teachers, charlatans, and spiritual con artists have infiltrated the church, seeking with their demonic doctrines to undermine the faith of genuine believers. They are doing Satan's bidding in the church. They present themselves as servants of righteousness, yet they are serving only themselves. Many of them sound very persuasive, blending lies with half-truths and emotional appeals—and they are carrying away many undiscerning followers to their spiritual destruction.

Truth is not determined by emotions. Truth is not determined by circumstances. Truth is not determined by the persuasiveness of a smooth-tongued teacher. Truth is determined by the Word of God.

SPIRITUAL SCAM ARTISTS

Some years ago, a prominent evangelical pastor was accused of engaging in homosexual practice and illegal drug abuse. At first, he denied the accusations. Then he abruptly resigned to undergo counseling under the supervision of four ministers. After three weeks of counseling, he declared himself free of homosexual feelings. Some in the church wanted to restore him immediately to the pulpit, while others, citing the biblical qualifications for church leadership in 1 Timothy 3 and Titus 1, insisted he was disqualified from pastoral ministry because he was not "above reproach, faithful to his wife, temperate, self-controlled, [or] respectable."

In the wake of the scandal, church attendance plummeted—and so did tithes and offerings. The church struggled to meet its financial obligations and considered laying off staff. Meanwhile, new accusations continued to surface against the former pastor. Although the church paid this pastor and his wife more than $300,000 in salary and benefits for more than a year after he resigned, he gave an ungrateful, self-pitying interview claiming "the church chose not to forgive me" and had told him to "go to hell."

In the months that followed, that church went through considerable soul-searching. The church leadership decided to take the congregation in a new direction, away from high-tech, big-screen Christian entertainment and toward a rediscovery of what it means to be a local, Bible-based church.

When a Christian leader sins and the church is gripped by scandal, it's important that the leaders and members of the church find a biblical balance of grace and truth. The Bible teaches that we should be gracious and loving for those who fall into sin—yet the Bible also teaches that leaders who violate God's clear standards for Christian leadership are disqualified from holding such positions. No leader who has brought scandal to the church should ever feel entitled to return to the pulpit—but as he seeks to be forgiven and restored in his marriage, a Bible-believing church will surround that fallen leader with Christian grace and love.

When a church is committed to living out the truth of God's Word, there is clarity, not confusion; there is purity, not pride; there is accountability, not permissiveness. A church that upholds God's truth will always give God the glory—not rob him of glory. When false teachers came to the church in Thessalonica, they came to steal the joy and peace of the Thessalonian believers. Paul wrote this letter to revive their joy and restore their peace.

In verse 3, Paul issues a strong command: "Don't let anyone deceive you in any way." In the original Greek, Paul uses a double negative, which serves to underscore and intensify this command. He wants the Thessalonians to understand the importance of guarding themselves against deception and false teaching.

Why is this so important? Paul explains: "for that day will not come until the rebellion occurs and the man of lawlessness is revealed, the man doomed to destruction." The end times could be upon us at any moment, without warning—and we all need to be spiritually prepared. When the antichrist is revealed, the world will become an incredibly dangerous and hostile place for Christians. Anyone who tolerates spiritual deception in his or her thinking will be taking a huge spiritual risk.

Paul wanted the Thessalonian believers to realize that listening to these spiritual scam artists actually placed their souls in jeopardy. What might seem like a small spiritual flaw could have enormous, eternal consequences. He didn't want his beloved brothers and sisters in Thessalonica to be caught unprepared for the sudden rise of the antichrist or the sudden return of the Lord Jesus Christ.

In verse 5, Paul says, "Don't you remember that when I was with you I used to tell you these things?" Paul is disappointed that so many of the Thessalonians had abandoned the teaching he had personally delivered to them. He had taught them that the day of the Lord would not come until the rebellion—the apostasy, the falling away—took place.

Paul knew that many in the church would fall away from the faith before the Lord's return. When Paul speaks of this coming "rebellion," the apostasy, he is saying there will be a full-fledged revolt against the truth among those who claim to be Christians. He is not describing mere ignorance of the truth—he's describing a revolution, a deliberate overthrow of the truth. Those who rebel against God's Word are not people who are ignorant of the gospel. They are those who have claimed to be Christians. They understand the way of salvation by grace through faith in Jesus Christ.

But they will defect from the church, and they will join the ranks of the enemy. They will be traitors to the cause of Christ. I believe this defection is already underway. These days, not a month goes by that I don't hear of some Christian leader, pastor, or author who has fallen away from the truth of the gospel. These defectors may still claim to be Christians, but they deny that Jesus is the only way to salvation.

In a letter to his spiritual son Timothy, Paul referred to such people as "having a form of godliness but denying its power"—then he added, "Have nothing to do with such people" (2 Timothy 3:5). They have moved from believing that Jesus is the way, the truth, and the life to believing that there are many paths to God. That's what it means to deny the power of godliness because it means denying the power of the gospel to save.

I'm not saying that the great apostasy Paul warns about is already here. But when that great apostasy begins, I want you to recognize it for what it is. And it is absolutely possible that we are seeing the first stirrings of that great apostasy even now.

It has become fashionable in many churches to say, "Yes, Jesus is my Savior—but that doesn't mean he's the only way to be saved." That sounds like such a harmless and broad-minded statement. It sounds so gracious and tolerant. But what that statement actually means is, "Jesus is a liar."

Do you find that shocking? I hope you do. To say that people can be saved apart from Jesus alone is a shocking statement—a statement that accuses Jesus of lying. Because Jesus himself said, "I am the way and the truth and the life. No one comes to the Father except through me" (John 14:6). Jesus clearly claims to be the one and only Savior of all mankind. You cannot contradict that claim without calling Jesus a liar.

This is how the small flaw of wanting to seem tolerant and open-minded leads us down the primrose path to heresy and apostasy. Jesus was not tolerant and open-minded when it came to his claims to be the Messiah and the Savior. He was quite narrow-minded on that score, which is why he said:

> "Enter through the narrow gate. For wide is the gate and broad is the road that leads to destruction, and many enter through it. But small is the gate and narrow the road that leads to life, and only a few find it" (Matthew 7:13-14).

If anyone ever calls you narrow-minded for staying true to the gospel, consider it a compliment. No authentic believer should ever want to be praised for being tolerant of error, falsehood, and sin.

"MANY ANTICHRISTS"

Notice that Paul draws a relationship between apostasy and the antichrist. Why does he do so? It's because apostasy will prepare the way for the antichrist. Apostasy will prepare the hearts of the masses to receive and worship the antichrist. Apostasy will create a climate in which the antichrist can reveal himself in all his satanic wickedness—and he will be applauded and embraced.

At first, the antichrist will pretend to be a godly leader, a friend to all nations, ethnicities, religions, and races. But when the time is right and he has solidified his power and popularity, he will drop all pretenses. He will reveal himself as an enemy of God, and he will demand to be worshiped as God.

When biblical absolutes are rejected even by churchgoers—

When the truth of salvation in Christ alone is mocked even by those who claim to be Christians—

When God's moral laws are torn down and replaced by tolerance for alternative lifestyles—

When preachers reject God's plan for marriage, replacing it with secularism and lawlessness—

Then the antichrist will be free to shed his disguise. He will not have to pretend to be moral. He will not have to pretend to be religious. He will not have to pretend to be sympathetic. All the moral and religious guardrails of humanity will be down. He will be free to do whatever he likes, and no one will stop him.

The antichrist will be free to persecute authentic biblical Christianity, knowing that he can do so without opposition and with the full approval and cooperation of the apostate church. Because apostasy has already infected the church and church leaders and churchgoers, the antichrist will be completely unopposed.

He will be revealed as the man of lawlessness, the one who is doomed to destruction. Did you know that the expression "the one doomed to destruction" is applied to only two people in the Bible? One is the antichrist. The other is Judas Iscariot.

Judas Iscariot spent three years at the side of Jesus, pretending to be a disciple. He was as close to the Son of God as all the other disciples.

He walked and talked with Jesus and was privileged to see and hear firsthand—

the sinlessness of Christ
the righteousness of Christ
the miracles of Christ
the teachings of Christ
the wisdom of Christ

In spite of all that he had seen and heard, Judas betrayed Jesus and sold him for thirty pieces of silver, the price of a slave. Judas betrayed the Son of God—and the antichrist will also be a betrayer. He will proclaim himself to be God and demand to be worshiped. Just as Judas defiled the temple with the blood money the priests paid him, the antichrist will desecrate the temple with the abomination that causes desolation.

The antichrist will also desecrate the temple of the Holy Spirit, the believers in whom the Spirit dwells. The antichrist will demand that they worship him—and those who refuse will be put to death.

And remember, the Bible does not warn us about just the coming of the antichrist. As the apostle John reminds us in 1 John 2:18, "even now many antichrists have come." There are many antichrists among us in our churches, but they do not belong to us and they do not teach the same gospel we believe.

Their teachings are subtle and persuasive. They seem so reasonable and compassionate. True, their message doesn't square with the Scriptures. They deny the claims of Christ. But isn't that just a small flaw?

These antichrists are preparing the way for *the* antichrist. They are preaching apostasy and heresy. Don't let anyone deceive you. The antichrist is coming to spread his shadow of deception over all the earth.

But if you put your faith in Jesus Christ as your Lord and Savior, you need not fear the antichrist—and you need not fear the Lord's return. When you see these signs—the spreading apostasy, the rebellion against God's truth, and the revealing of the antichrist—you know that the day of your redemption is drawing nigh.

We don't fear the forces of darkness because we are children of the light.

12

THE RESTRAINT OF EVIL

2 Thessalonians 2:6-12

W hen I was a boy growing up in Egypt, our home was protected by guard dogs. They were not huggable pets, they were *attack dogs*. They were huge animals, and if you stood them up on their hind legs, they were six feet tall from snout to hind paws. Those dogs were also extremely territorial, and no one could go near them except my father. He was the only human being they trusted.

My father would rise early every morning and tie up the dogs so that our family and any visitors would be safe. Late at night, he would go out and set the dogs loose to roam freely on our property.

On one occasion, an intruder came to our home late at night to steal from us. The guard dogs intercepted him and mauled him. The sight of that bloodied man is etched in my memory to this day. That incident makes it abundantly clear why our guard dogs had to be chained up and restrained during the day. Those animals were too dangerous to run loose among innocent, unsuspecting people. If they had not been restrained during the day, no one but my father could have gone in or out of our house.

When I think of how my father used to restrain our attack dogs, I'm reminded of this passage in Paul's second letter to the Thessalonians:

> And now you know what is holding him back, so that he
> may be revealed at the proper time. For the secret power of

lawlessness is already at work; but the one who now holds it back will continue to do so till he is taken out of the way. And then the lawless one will be revealed, whom the Lord Jesus will overthrow with the breath of his mouth and destroy by the splendor of his coming (2 Thessalonians 2:6-8).

Here the apostle Paul gives us a word picture of how God restrains what he calls "the secret power of lawlessness," the power of the antichrist. God is restraining evil—for now.

When you look around at the horrors and atrocities taking place all around the world, you might be tempted to wonder if evil is being restrained at all. But if God were not actively holding back, holding down, and suppressing Satan and his power, you would witness nothing less than the end of the world. A day will come when God will remove the present restraints, and the world will see tyranny, violence, war, and slaughter on a scale we can scarcely imagine.

Down through the years, students of the Bible have speculated about how God restrains evil in the world. In verse 6, Paul speaks of this restraining power in the neuter gender, suggesting that the restraining power is a force, not a person.

This has led some people to theorize that the restraining power that holds back evil is *the preaching of the gospel*. People who hold this view often point to the Lord's prophetic statement in Matthew 24:14: "And this gospel of the kingdom will be preached in the whole world as a testimony to all nations, and then the end will come." Once the gospel has been preached to every nation, they say, this restraint will be removed, the antichrist will be revealed, and the end of the world will come.

Other Bible scholars suggest that the force that restrains evil in the world today is the church, which acts as salt and light. Others suggest that the restraining force is the nation of Israel. Others, including my late friend John Stott, believe that the restraining force is government, which has been ordained by God to curtail evil. According to this view, when there is no government, when the social order collapses, then the antichrist will appear.

Still others have said that the restraining power that holds back evil is the archangel Michael, who is shown battling demonic forces in Daniel 10. Yet in Jude verse 9, we learn that Michael did not dare to take on Satan himself, but instead told the devil, "The Lord rebuke you!"

If the archangel Michael is not sufficiently strong to overpower Satan, then how could humans hope to restrain the evil of the antichrist? The antichrist will be possessed by Satan and empowered by Satan. Human beings won't stand a chance against the antichrist.

Human beings preach the gospel. Human beings make up the nation of Israel. Human beings make up the government. Human beings make up the church—and the church is not able to restrain evil even within its own walls. No human being, no human agency, no human activity can hope to contain or restrain the power of Satan.

In verse 7, Paul speaks of this restraining power in the masculine gender, suggesting that the restraining power is in fact a *Person*. Only one power can restrain Satan and Satan's human puppet, the antichrist—*the power of God himself.*

It is God alone who says to Satan, "You can go thus far but no further. You can test Job with illness, loss, and sorrow—but don't take his life. You can sift Peter like wheat, but I won't permit you to destroy him." God draws boundaries that Satan is forbidden to trespass. And while Satan is free to roam the earth and cause incredible suffering, sin, and destruction, he can operate only within the limits God has set.

Satan does not like being pinned down to God's timetable, unable to carry out all the evil plans he can imagine. He doesn't like being restrained by the sovereignty, authority, and power of God. He wants nothing more than to reveal his false Messiah so that he can usurp God's glory.

But we should always remember that Jesus has his foot on Satan's neck, and there's nothing Satan can do about it. As Job said to God, "I know that you can do all things; no purpose of yours can be thwarted" (Job 42:2). The man of lawlessness will appear on God's timetable, not Satan's. God will keep him restrained until all of his redeemed have entered salvation's gate.

One of the great tragedies of the church is that so many believers give Satan more credit than he deserves. They think he is more powerful than he really is. They live in fear of Satan. Whenever something goes wrong in their lives—even the natural consequences of disobedience—they say, "Oh, Satan is attacking me!" Please understand: Not every problem, setback, or annoyance is the work of Satan. Some Christians struggle with a habit or an addiction or a recurring temptation, and they say, "We need to bind Satan!" In most cases, we simply need to live in dependence on God.

We have many confused Christians running from church to church, from preacher to preacher, from teacher to teacher, looking for answers to the "satanic attacks" they are suffering. In many cases, Satan simply has them stampeded. He doesn't have to attack them—he enjoys watching them run around in panic, thinking that he's chasing them. The real answer to their spiritual problems is obedience!

I'm not saying we don't have to be wary of Satan. We do. But we should be careful not to ascribe more power to Satan then he deserves. Much of the temptation we experience comes from the flesh, from our own undisciplined thoughts and ungodly desires. If we would bring our thoughts into captivity before God, if we would truly cast our cares upon him, these temptations would no longer have a toehold in our lives.

"TAKEN OUT OF THE WAY"

Paul says in verse 7, "For the secret power of lawlessness is already at work; but the one who now holds it back will continue to do so till he is taken out of the way." Satan's power works in secret, and those who live in darkness cannot see it. Satan's workings are a mystery to them. But we who live in the light of God's truth can see the secret power of Satan at work in the world. The evidence of satanic lawlessness is no secret to us. We see it operating everywhere.

We see satanic lawlessness operating in our government. We see it operating in our schools, in our workplace, in our neighborhood. We see the activity of lying spirits infiltrating our society, spreading lies about God and godliness throughout our media, our culture, and the people all around us.

We see an increasing double standard in our schools today, all the way down to the kindergarten level. Many public schools now require students to learn the Five Pillars of Islam in the name of "tolerance and understanding," while banning the Judeo-Christian Ten Commandments in the name of "separation of church and state." Many elementary schools and high schools promote the acceptance of homosexuality and how-to classes on "safe sex" and "outercourse" while banning the teaching of abstinence and traditional morality.

Where does this kind of inverted logic come from? Why do our educational systems teach that up is down, good is evil, and morality is immoral? It's because "the secret power of lawlessness is already at work." But when the One who restrains lawlessness is taken out of the way, the secret power of Satan will be a secret no longer. It will be right out in the open.

Right now, immorality creeps quietly in the dark corners of millions of hearts in millions of homes. False religions are silently infiltrating our social and educational institutions. But when the man of lawlessness is finally revealed, all the evil that operates in secret will suddenly explode like a thermonuclear bomb. Evil will spread across the globe at the speed of light. All the restraints that are now in place will be gone.

It will be hell on earth.

Look again at the second half of verse 7: "but the one who now holds it back will continue to do so till he is taken out of the way." Paul speaks of a Person—an unnamed Person who will be "taken out of the way." Here Paul uses the masculine pronoun. He can be referring to only one Person, and that is the Holy Spirit of God.

The Holy Spirit is the supernatural Spirit who holds Satan in check. The Holy Spirit is the supernatural Spirit who restrains wickedness. The Holy Spirit is the supernatural Spirit who said in Genesis 6:3, "My Spirit will not contend with humans forever." The Holy Spirit is the supernatural Spirit who opposes evil, convicts the world of sin, and empowers believers to obey God and resist temptation.

It's important to note that Paul does not say that the Holy Spirit disappears from the world. He does not say that the Holy Spirit ceases to exist in the world. He says that the Holy Spirit will be taken out of the way.

It is as if the Holy Spirit guards a door that Satan is trying to enter. Satan can pound on the door, ram his shoulder into the door, and try to kick the door in—but the Holy Spirit is too powerful for Satan to overcome. But one day, in God's timing, as Satan is trying to force his way through that door, the Holy Spirit will simply step aside. He will be taken out of the way—and Satan will plow through that door unopposed.

At that moment, the reign of the antichrist will begin. His reign, however, will be short-lived. As Paul writes in verse 8, "And then the lawless one will be revealed, whom the Lord Jesus will overthrow with the breath of his mouth and destroy by the splendor of his coming." There will be no long, drawn-out battle, no protracted warfare. Victory will be swift, even instantaneous. Victory will be immediate—and eternal.

A POWERFUL DELUSION

But the question remains: How will the antichrist succeed in deceiving millions, even billions of people into following and worshipping him? Surely, great masses of people will recognize him as completely evil, and they will reject him, won't they? Paul answers these questions in verses 9 to 12:

> The coming of the lawless one will be in accordance with how Satan works. He will use all sorts of displays of power through signs and wonders that serve the lie, and all the ways that wickedness deceives those who are perishing. They perish because they refused to love the truth and so be saved. For this reason God sends them a powerful delusion so that they will believe the lie and so that all will be condemned who have not believed the truth but have delighted in wickedness (2 Thessalonians 2:9-12).

The antichrist will have an array of supernatural powers given to him by Satan. The Greek word Paul uses for "power" is *energeia*.

Throughout the Scriptures, this word is most often used to speak of God's power and activity. But Paul chose this word with care because Satan will energize the antichrist with demonic power so that he can imitate the miracles of God with fake, demonic miracles. Satan's puppet will perform counterfeit signs and wonders to deceive undiscerning people. Because of these signs and wonders, most of the world will believe in him, thinking that he is the second coming of Christ.

One of the chief reasons people will be fooled by the antichrist's deception is that the minds of the masses will have already been deluded by global apostasy. Because people have already rejected the truth about Jesus, it will be easy for the antichrist to deceive them with his lies. Jesus himself prophesied about the end times, "For false messiahs and false prophets will appear and perform great signs and wonders to deceive, if possible, even the elect" (Matthew 24:24).

Those who don't stand for the truth about the Lord Jesus Christ will fall for the lie of the antichrist. Those who are not anchored in Christ alone will fall for the magic tricks and special effects of the antichrist. Those who demand "signs and wonders" in order to believe will reject the Christ of the cross—and will follow the antichrist into hell.

Those who do not base their faith on the truth of Scripture will bet their eternal destiny on a satanic deception. They have made their choice. They will have no excuse when they face the final judgment.

Paul writes, "For this reason God sends them a powerful delusion." For *what* reason? *Why* does God send these unbelievers a powerful delusion? Because, Paul says, "they refused to love the truth and so be saved." They have refused to believe that salvation is through Jesus Christ and his cross alone. They have tried to reach God by some other path, by some other religion, and perhaps by a religion of their own making. They have refused the salvation freely offered to them by grace through faith in Christ.

You might say, "Is that really fair? How can God send these people a 'powerful delusion'? Shouldn't he give them one last chance to receive the truth?" But there is a principle in the Bible, from Genesis to Revelation, that if a person adamantly rejects God and his plan of salvation, God says, "Have it your way. I will give you what you want—and

I'll give you *more* of what you want. If you choose to be deluded, then fine, you can have your delusions—in fact, here is even *more* delusion."

In the book of Exodus, when Moses went to Pharaoh and demanded that he liberate the Hebrew people, Pharaoh hardened his heart and refused to let them go. God watched as Pharaoh dug in his heels and refused to budge—and God said, in effect, "Have it your way, Pharaoh. If you choose to be hardhearted toward my chosen people, I will send you even more hardness of heart." Ultimately, Pharaoh reaped anguish and suffering because of his choice, because God sent plague after plague as punishment for his rejection of God's demand. The final and ultimate plague took the life of Pharaoh's own son.

In the first chapter of Romans, Paul writes about the godlessness and wickedness of the human race, which has knowingly and willfully rejected the truth about God. Three times in this chapter Paul says, "God gave them over."

- "Therefore God gave them over in the sinful desires of their hearts to sexual impurity" (verse 24).

- "Because of this, God gave them over to shameful lusts" (verse 26).

- "So God gave them over to a depraved mind" (verse 28).

Why did God give sinful human beings over to sexual impurity, lust, and depravity? Because of their rebellious spirit. Because of their unrepentant hearts. Because of their willful disobedience. The opposite of believing the truth is delighting in wickedness. The truth makes moral demands. The truth has moral implications. The truth brings conviction and transformation.

The root of the human problem is not just erroneous thinking. As Paul says, "For since the creation of the world God's invisible qualities—his eternal power and divine nature—have been clearly seen, being understood from what has been made, so that people are without excuse" (Romans 1:20). Even atheists and agnostics, even Islamists and New Agers, even the religious and the irreligious know enough about God's nature, as revealed in creation, to be without excuse.

So the human problem—as Paul lays it out with a grim, inexorable logic in Romans 1—is not mere erroneous thinking. The problem is a *deliberate choice* to do evil. People know the truth, they reject the truth, they deliberately choose evil, and they delight in evil. They have had their chance to choose God. They rejected that offer—so God hands them over to their own evil desires and their own self-delusion.

Thus they are condemned for all eternity.

THE NIGHT IS COMING

My friend, this is a serious matter. I can't imagine any issue in your life that is more important. It is impossible to love the truth and love evil at the same time. If you love one, you will hate the other. There is no other option. Each of us needs to take stock of our lives and ask ourselves: Do I love the truth? Or do I love sin?

There is a five-stage regression down a horrible slippery slope that leads to our spiritual destruction. Those five steps are:

- We willfully choose the pleasures of sin.

- Having chosen the love of sin, we reject God's truth.

- Having rejected God's truth, we invite the deception of Satan.

- Because we are willfully self-deceived and deceived by Satan, God gives us over to our sin and delusion and the hardening of our hearts.

- All of this culminates in eternal condemnation and regret.

How can we escape being dragged down this slippery slope to destruction? There is only one way out: Love the truth. Embrace the truth. Cling to the truth for dear life.

That's why Jesus said, "I am the way and the truth and the life." If you don't want to be drawn downward to destruction by the moral gravity of depravity, Jesus is the only way. If you don't want to be deluded by your deceitful lusts and the lies of Satan, Jesus is the only truth. If you don't want to suffer the pain and regret of eternal death, Jesus is the only pathway to life.

Right now, we all have a very narrow window of opportunity—the window of our own mortal existence. None of us knows how wide that window is—if it is the span of thirty or sixty or ninety years. During that short span, we will determine our eternal destiny by the choices we make and the truths we believe or the truths we reject.

At this present moment, we are living in the daytime—a time when God is restraining Satan, restraining the antichrist, restraining the full onslaught of demonic evil. God is restraining these evil forces just as my father restrained those attack dogs during the daytime.

But a time is coming when all the restraints will be removed. When the nighttime of history arrives, it will be too late to alter our choices and accept the truth. When the savage animals are let loose upon the world, those who remain will have no way of escape.

Now is the time for repenting and turning to God. Now is the time when anyone who wants to turn to the Lord may do so. Now is the time when no one will be turned away.

Don't wait for the nighttime of lawlessness to descend. Don't wait for the man of lawlessness to be revealed. Don't wait for the time of retribution to begin.

The time is coming when God will judge those who have rejected the truth and believed the lie of the antichrist. This is the endgame of God's program for history. Which side will you be on?

13

STANDING FIRM WHEN ALL HELL BREAKS LOOSE

2 Thessalonians 2:13-17

I t was an amazing experience, some years ago, to witness the construction of our church campus. I was especially intrigued as I watched the workers laying the foundation for our parking deck.

The work began with the digging of holes for the steel and concrete support columns. These were massive columns, about a dozen feet in diameter. As I watched the holes being dug, I noticed that they were all of equal diameter but varying depths. Some of the holes were dug to a depth of about eight feet. Others were twenty feet deep or more.

So I asked one of the construction managers why these holes were not all the same depth. I'll never forget his answer. He said, "Do you want a stable parking deck that is strong enough to support all the cars and people it must hold?"

"Absolutely," I said.

"The reason those columns are sunk to different depths is that we keep digging until we find solid rock. Sometimes, we find rock at a depth of eight feet. Sometimes, we find rock at a depth of twenty feet or more. The depth of the rock determines the depth of the hole. As long as the support columns are resting on rock, the entire structure will be stable."

Stability is vitally important to a parking structure, and it's vitally important in every other sphere of life. An orderly civilization depends on maintaining a stable government. Commerce and prosperity require a stable economy. Ships, submarines, and aircraft use stabilizing surfaces to counteract turbulence and maintain a safe and smooth voyage. Parents need to provide a stable home in order for children to grow up emotionally strong and healthy.

I once read that the nuclear aircraft carrier *USS Eisenhower* has four and a half acres of flight deck, a displacement of 95,000 tons, and can launch sixty aircraft. It has not one but two anchors, each weighing 60,000 pounds, and each with a chain that is 1,082 feet long. Each link of the anchor chain weighs 365 pounds. The *Eisenhower* is built for stability. It's designed to give a smooth ride even in rough and stormy seas. A warship that must launch its aircraft at a moment's notice cannot be tossed about by the elements. It must be a stable platform under any conditions—and the *Eisenhower* meets that daunting requirement.

Stability! We all want to live stable, predictable lives without having to deal with nasty surprises. Unfortunately, this fallen world does not afford much stability. Circumstances change. Obstacles arise. Opposition invades our lives. When trouble comes, when the seas of life turn rough and stormy, our stability as believers is tested. Will we be tossed about by the storms? Or will we remain stable, firm, and anchored in the Lord Jesus?

That is the question the apostle Paul addresses in the next section of his second letter to the Thessalonians.

"STAND FIRM AND HOLD FAST"

The New Testament is replete with exhortations to stand firm and maintain a stable faith. Jesus told his disciples that when persecution comes, "Stand firm, and you will win life" (Luke 21:19).

Paul included encouragement to "stand firm" in most of his letters. For example, writing to the Corinthians, he said, "Therefore, my dear brothers and sisters, stand firm. Let nothing move you" (1 Corinthians 15:58). To the believers in Ephesus he wrote, "Stand firm then, with the belt of truth buckled around your waist, with the breastplate of righteousness in place" (Ephesians 6:14). And he urged the Christians in Colossae to "continue in your faith, established and firm, and do not move from the hope held out in the gospel" (Colossians 1:23).

The apostle James also placed great emphasis on stability and standing firm. He urged all believers to pray confidently, never doubting, because those who lack confidence in prayer are "double-minded and unstable in all they do" (James 1:8). He urged believers to maintain a stable and persistent faith, saying, "be patient and stand firm, because the Lord's coming is near" (James 5:8).

And the apostle Peter urged believers to remain stable and unyielding whenever Satan attacks: "Resist him, standing firm in the faith, because you know that the family of believers throughout the world is undergoing the same kind of sufferings" (1 Peter 5:9).

Here in 2 Thessalonians 2, Paul urges the believers in Thessalonica "not to become easily unsettled or alarmed" by false teachings that were infiltrating the church. And in the closing verses of chapter 2, Paul again exhorts these believers to maintain a stable faith that does not sway in the shifting winds of false teachings:

> But we ought always to thank God for you, brothers and sisters loved by the Lord, because God chose you as firstfruits to be saved through the sanctifying work of the Spirit and through belief in the truth. He called you to this through our gospel, that you might share in the glory of our Lord Jesus Christ.
>
> So then, brothers and sisters, stand firm and hold fast to the teachings we passed on to you, whether by word of mouth or by letter.
>
> May our Lord Jesus Christ himself and God our Father, who loved us and by his grace gave us eternal encouragement and good hope, encourage your hearts and strengthen you in every good deed and word (2 Thessalonians 2:13-17).

Here Paul pleads with the Thessalonian believers not to listen to unsound doctrines but to "stand firm and hold fast to the teachings we passed on to you." How can Christians be made stable in their beliefs? How can they stand firm? Especially in these days, when we are surrounded by so many conflicting ideas about truth and spiritual reality, how can we find stability and the rock-solid place to make our stand?

In a real sense, the Thessalonian church was like a ship being tossed on a raging ocean. These believers needed an anchor to keep from being tossed about by the turbulence of shifting opinions and the storms of life. They faced pounding waves of persecution. They faced storm billows of false teaching. So Paul told them he was praying for them—especially for their spiritual stability. He was praying that they would stand firm on the teachings he had delivered to them.

Paul's prayer was not merely for one local congregation in one coastal city in northern Greece. His prayer extends to all believers in all places in all times who face the destabilizing forces of trials, persecutions, and false teachers. Above all, he prayed for those who would have to face the antichrist, who would experience the end-times upheaval when all hell breaks loose. In that time of lawlessness, anarchy, terror, and unrestrained evil, believers will need supernatural strength and God-given stability in order to stand firm.

Paul reminds them of the anchor that holds them as strong and secure as the 60,000-pound anchor of a nuclear aircraft carrier. He reminds them of the bedrock of truth that keeps them firmly in place. He reminds them of the unshakable hope and encouragement they have in the gospel of Jesus Christ.

"We ought always to thank God for you, brothers and sisters loved by the Lord." Why? Because they are nice people? Because they are tolerant and understanding of alternative lifestyles? Because they fit right in with their pagan neighbors? Because they have mastered the art of compromise? No, Paul says "because God chose you as firstfruits to be saved through the sanctifying work of the Spirit and through belief in the truth."

The world will applaud you when you compromise your beliefs and water down the gospel. But Jesus will reward you if you hold fast to the truth and stand firm on the gospel. Paul gives thanks because God chose and called these believers to be saved—and God will bring them safely all the way home. God will guide them through the turbulence of persecution. God will anchor their faith through storms of testing and trouble. God will be their fortress when the man of lawlessness is revealed.

Jesus has given us this same assurance:

> "All those the Father gives me will come to me, and whoever comes to me I will never drive away...And this is the will of him who sent me, that I shall lose none of all those he has given me, but raise them up at the last day. For my Father's will is that everyone who looks to the Son and believes in him shall have eternal life, and I will raise them up at the last day" (John 6:37,39-40).

And that's not all! Jesus also said:

> "My sheep listen to my voice; I know them, and they follow me. I give them eternal life, and they shall never perish; no one will snatch them out of my hand. My Father, who has given them to me, is greater than all; no one can snatch them out of my Father's hand" (John 10:27-29).

If these statements from the lips of our Lord himself don't give you all the stability you need in life, I don't know what will. This truth alone should keep us in a perpetual state of thanksgiving and praise.

GOD'S SOVEREIGN CALLING

In this passage, Paul also contrasts the redeemed with the unredeemed. As we've seen, the unredeemed are those who love sin, hate the truth, and follow the antichrist. As a result, God gave them over to their delusions and they are eternally condemned.

But here, in the closing verses of chapter 2, Paul gives us a contrasting description of the redeemed. As believers, we are being sanctified by the Spirit, we love and hold fast to the truth, we follow Christ himself, and as a result, God has given us an eternal encouragement and a great hope, and we will share in the glory of the Lord Jesus Christ! And all of this is a result of God's grace and sovereign choice. As Paul tells us, "He called you to this through our gospel" (verse 14).

When did God choose you? When did God call you? Was it when you realized for the first time that you were a sinner and you needed a Savior? Was it when you first went to your knees and invited him to be the Lord of your life? No. He called you before you were born, before your parents and grandparents were born. He called you—are you ready for this?—*before the foundation of the world.*

That's not my opinion. That is what Paul tells us in God's Word: "For he chose us in him before the creation of the world to be holy and blameless in his sight" (Ephesians 1:4). The future, the present, and the past are all the same to God. He looked down the timeline of the history of the universe, and he saw you long before you were born. He knew you and he loved you. He called you and he chose you. Understand, he didn't choose you because you are so lovable. If anything, you are lovable *only* because God chose you and his Spirit is performing his sanctifying work in your life.

And because of God's love for us, because he chose us when there was nothing lovable about us and we were lost in our sin, we should want to live to please him. And every time we sin, every time we displease him, we should feel pangs of remorse and regret, realizing how much we have hurt the One who loves us and saved us. Why should we ever want to offend and disappoint such divine and eternal Love?

God's grace toward us is a reflection of who he is. He reached down into our lives when we were hopelessly damaged, completely worthless, sin-stained and unfit for any purpose. He healed us, invested his life in us, cleansed our stains, and set us apart for his purpose. The value we now have is the value he poured into us.

The Lord chose you and me in the same sovereign way he chose Israel in the Old Testament. As Moses told the ungrateful, complaining, murmuring Israelites, "The LORD did not set his affection on you and choose you because you were more numerous than other peoples, for you were the fewest of all peoples" (Deuteronomy 7:7). In other words, God chose the Israelites in spite of who they were, not because of who they were.

If God were looking for the most brilliant, accomplished go-getters on the planet, he would have chosen the Egyptians. They had built the most advanced civilization of that era. In the same way, God could have his pick of the most brilliant scientists, the most beautiful actors and supermodels, the most powerful athletes, the most gifted orators. But that's not how God chooses his followers.

God is sovereign, loving, and caring—and the way he chooses us demolishes our pride and ego. His sovereign choice of you and me ensures that God gets all the credit for salvation. He alone is exalted. He alone receives the glory and praise. His sovereign and undeserved love produces joy and gratitude in our hearts. We feel privileged and amazed that he would choose us and love us. His holiness makes our lives stable and secure.

Some people claim that the doctrine of God's sovereign choosing undermines our zeal for witnessing to others about Christ. They think that if God is sovereign, why should we have to witness? God will choose whomever he wants, and no amount of evangelism on our part can ever affect God's sovereign choice.

That's the wrong way to look at spiritual reality. Yes, God sovereignly chooses his followers—but he has given us the privilege and joy of participating with him in calling the lost to himself. God has made us partners with him in carrying out his eternal plan of salvation.

Remember what Paul told the Thessalonians: "He called you to this *through our gospel*, that you might share in the glory of our Lord Jesus Christ." God called the Thessalonians to himself—not by skywriting a message in the clouds, not with handwriting on the wall, and not with a voice in their heads. God called them through the gospel that Paul himself shared with them. God used Paul as his partner in ministry, his messenger of the good news. And Paul felt honored and privileged to be God's ambassador to the Thessalonians.

When we have a biblical understanding of God's sovereign calling, it fills us with a sense of gratitude. We feel honored that God can use us to bring others into his kingdom. We feel grateful for the privilege of being his ambassadors of the gospel. And we want to tell everyone we meet about the greatest treasure ever discovered—the treasure of eternal life through Jesus Christ.

THE EVIDENCE OF HISTORY

Paul is making a powerful point. He is telling us that the very fact that God has sovereignly, lovingly chosen us should banish fear from our lives—especially the fear of sharing Christ with others. Let Satan do his worst. Let the man of lawlessness be revealed. Let the persecution began. Let all hell break loose!

We will not be shaken.

We will not be moved.

We will not be intimidated.

We will stand firm, confident in the certainty that we are held securely in the palm of his hand. We are cradled in his arms, and anyone who touches us touches the apple of his eye.

There is no stability or security in our circumstances. There is only stability and security in the sovereignty of God's loving choice. That is why Paul is able to say to the Thessalonians and to us, "Stand firm." After he has given us all the evidences for holding on to our faith, he then appeals to all believers to stand firm in the truth of the gospel.

Today, we hear many motivational teachers and preachers offering empty affirmations: "If you believe in yourself, you can do it!" "If you can dream it, you can accomplish it!" "If life hands you lemons, make lemonade!" The problem with these slogans is that they are all focused on you, you, *you*. No wonder so many followers of the motivational gurus end up defeated and discouraged.

If the foundation of your confidence is you, then you have built your life on a very shaky foundation. Imagine if the support columns of our parking structure rested on shifting sand instead of solid bedrock. Sand provides no support, no security, no stability. Building your life on a foundation of your own self-confidence is like building on sand. But building your life on the solid rock of the Lord Jesus Christ will bring you stability and security. You will stand firm, you will be anchored securely.

How do you build your life on the solid rock of Jesus Christ? By holding on to something that is secure and immovable. That's why Paul says, "Stand firm and hold fast to the teachings we passed on to you, whether by word of mouth or by letter" (verse 15). Those teachings—the truth of the gospel, the foundation of the Christian faith as it was handed to us from Jesus—are your anchor in the storm. Those teachings are the rock-solid foundation of your faith. They consist of the historical evidence of:

- Christ's life
- Christ's teaching
- Christ's miraculous work
- Christ's identity as the Son of God
- Christ's redeeming death on the cross
- Christ's resurrection on the third day
- Christ's ascension into heaven
- Christ's promise to come back and judge the world

The stability of our faith is rooted in the rock-solid evidence of the Lord Jesus and the salvation he obtained for us upon the cross. Our security is based on God's sovereign choice and unconditional love for us.

Paul concludes this chapter with a prayer that the God of power might comfort and strengthen those Thessalonian Christians—and Christians at all times, in all places. His prayer teaches us an all-important lesson: Our stability, our ability to stand firm on the good news of Christ, rests on the foundation of God's unchanging love.

May we never take his love for granted. May we never be like those who just coast through the Christian life, resting on their blessed assurance, making no effort to win the lost or advance the kingdom of God. The Lord has called us to carry out an important mission in a dangerous world, and he has given us the power to complete our mission.

We cannot carry out our mission in our own strength. We cannot serve the Lord and serve others in our own strength. We cannot spread the good news of Jesus Christ and attract people into his kingdom in our own strength. We need to live in total dependence on his strength—or we will crash and burn.

William Wilberforce (1759–1833) was an evangelical Christian politician in England. He led the movement to abolish the slave trade in the British Empire. It was a long and discouraging political battle with many setbacks. After a decade as a member of Parliament, trying without success to end the practice of chattel slavery, Wilberforce felt discouraged and defeated. He took his Bible and sat down to read a passage for comfort and strength. As he opened the Bible, a sheet of paper fell out—a letter he had tucked into those pages years before.

Wilberforce picked up the letter and began reading. It was a letter that evangelist John Wesley had written to him years earlier. They were the last words Wesley ever wrote. The great preacher had penned them with his ebbing strength as he lay on his deathbed, just six days before his death. The letter, dated February 24, 1791, read:

> Unless the divine power has raised you up...I see not how you can go through your glorious enterprise in opposing that execrable villainy [of slavery], which is the scandal of religion, of England, and of human nature. Unless God has raised you up for this very thing, you will be worn out by the opposition of men and devils. But if God be for you, who can be against you? Are all of them stronger than God? O be not weary of well-doing! Go on, in the name of God and in the power of His might, till even American slavery (the vilest that ever saw the sun) shall vanish away before it...
>
> That He who has guided you from youth up may continue to strengthen you in this and all things is the prayer of, dear sir,
>
> > Your affectionate servant,
> > John Wesley[32]

Those words—written years earlier with John Wesley's last ounces of strength—gave Wilberforce the power to go on. It was a long and tortuous journey to his goal. It wasn't until 1833 that Parliament finally passed the Slavery Abolition Act, which ended slavery throughout the British Empire. Wilberforce lived to see the achievement of his dream. He died just three days after hearing that the Act was passed—after spending *the last forty-six years of his life* in the pursuit of that goal.

The words of Wesley that inspired and motivated William Wilberforce are important words for your life and mine: If God be for you, who can be against you? Go on, in the name of God and in the power of his might. He who has guided you in the past will continue to be your strength.

The power of God enables us to stand firm in the faith. The strength of God will sustain us in the stormy days ahead.

14

A TWO-WAY
CONVERSATION WITH GOD

2 Thessalonians 3:1-5

W hen I travel, I regularly encounter people I have never met before and will likely never see again this side of heaven. And they often say to me something that deeply touches my heart: "I pray for you and your ministry every single day."

There's no way I can express to them the depth of my gratitude for their prayers. There's no way I can adequately thank the Lord for bringing such people into my life. I believe that the effectiveness of any Christian ministry is directly proportional to the prayers of the saints.

Why does prayer make such a difference? Couldn't God do all that he's doing around the world without our prayers? Isn't God able to bless ministries, touch lives, heal broken hearts, and call lost souls to himself without our prayers? Of course he could. He is God. He doesn't *need* our prayers.

And yet, God has chosen to involve us, mere fallen human beings, in his eternal plan for history. He doesn't need us—but he *loves* us. He doesn't need us—but he *chooses* us. He doesn't need us—but he *involves* us in the all-important work he is doing. And in some mysterious way that is far beyond human understanding, he accomplishes his work through our prayers.

Obviously, the power of prayer does not reside in us; it's God's power alone. But God has designed the universe in such a way that the prayers of God's people draw upon the sovereign power of God. The result: Prayer changes things. Prayer makes big things happen. This is a biblical principle.

Again and again, we see how the apostle Paul expresses dependence on—and gratitude for—the prayers of the saints. We see this most clearly in the first five verses of 2 Thessalonians 3:

> As for other matters, brothers and sisters, pray for us that the message of the Lord may spread rapidly and be honored, just as it was with you. And pray that we may be delivered from wicked and evil people, for not everyone has faith. But the Lord is faithful, and he will strengthen you and protect you from the evil one. We have confidence in the Lord that you are doing and will continue to do the things we command. May the Lord direct your hearts into God's love and Christ's perseverance (2 Thessalonians 3:1-5).

In this letter, Paul has been peering into the future—giving us a glimpse of the revelation of the Lord Jesus Christ on the last day of history, foreshadowing the withdrawal of the Holy Spirit's restraining power, foretelling the unleashing of the full force of the spirit of lawlessness upon the world, forewarning us of the rise of the antichrist. Then, after describing these future events, Paul proceeds to tell us how we should live in the meantime.

Today, we are living out our lives in the gap between the two comings of Jesus Christ. His first advent occurred more than two thousand years ago. His next advent will take place at a date and time known only to God the Father. How should we, as believers, pray as we await the second coming of Christ?

In 2 Thessalonians 2, Paul urged us to hold fast to the truth of the Word of God. Today, we see many ministers, theologians, and bestselling authors compromising God's truth and abandoning it altogether. Like Esau of old, they are selling their spiritual birthright for the equivalent of a pot of soup: popularity, friendship with the world, and praise for being open-minded and inclusive.

Now more than ever, we need to be authentically Christian, holding fast to the truth, standing firm for the truth, remaining 100 percent immovable when it comes to biblical truth. There is nothing in this world more important than the truth of God's Word. That's why, here in 2 Thessalonians 3:1, Paul tells us to pray that this same Word of God "may spread rapidly and be honored" throughout the world and culture of that day.

We need an outpouring of that same kind of prayer today.

THE FOCUS OF OUR PRAYERS

The vision statement of our church reads: "Reaching the Lost and Equipping the Saints for the Work of Ministry." The first part of that statement—"Reaching the Lost"—expresses our prayerful desire that the Word of God "may spread rapidly" throughout our world. The second part—"Equipping the Saints for the Work of Ministry"—speaks of our prayerful desire that the Word of God "be honored" and instilled into the life of every believer. There is no escaping the biblical urgency of these two foundational pillars of our faith. Every ministry, every program, and every outreach we engage in must be based on these two essential foundation stones, reaching the lost and equipping the saints.

The apostle Paul, too, was committed to reaching the lost and equipping the saints. His chief desire was that the Word of God spread rapidly throughout the world and that it be honored and instilled in the lives of the saints. Paul had no equal in intellectual brilliance, rabbinic education, insightful logic, persuasive speech, and spiritual perception. He was an experienced missionary, preacher, and strategist. But his effectiveness for Christ was not rooted in any of these human traits and abilities. It was rooted in his total dependence on the power of the Lord Jesus Christ and the life that Christ lived through him.

As Paul told the believers in Colossae, "To this end I strenuously contend with all the energy Christ so powerfully works in me" (Colossians 1:29). And to the Galatians he said, "I have been crucified with Christ and I no longer live, but Christ lives in me. The life I now live in the body, I live by faith in the Son of God, who loved me and gave himself for me" (Galatians 2:20). Paul knew that in his own strength, he could accomplish nothing for God. The effectiveness of his ministry was based solely on his availability to God—his willingness to allow the life of Christ to work through him.

That's why he repeatedly asked believers to pray for him and his ministry. He wanted his fellow Christians to ask God to do a mighty work through him. Paul himself took no credit for all the people who were converted through his preaching or all the churches that were planted through his labors. He gave all the glory to the Lord Jesus Christ, and he urgently pleaded for the Thessalonian believers to bathe his missionary work in prayer.

Do we still believe in prayer today? Well, in a way. Many Christians are willing to pray fervently for wealth and health and a big new house and a shiny new car. They are willing to pray for a promotion or for good weather on their vacation. But how many of those eager prayer warriors are also praying for the fulfillment of the Great Commission, for the protection of believers who are being persecuted, for the effectiveness of evangelistic ministries at home and abroad? Are we great intercessors, going to spiritual war against the invisible principalities and powers of Satan? Or are we simply immature children asking our Daddy in heaven to give us the goodies we want?

There is nothing wrong with pouring out our wants and needs before the Lord. But if selfish prayers are the sum total of our prayer life, then we have a stunted and immature prayer life. There is nothing wrong with saying to God, "Lord, I'm facing a crisis!" or "Lord, my loved ones need your help!" But we have to ask ourselves if it's true that God hears from us only when we're in trouble—and if that's true, what does that say about our love for God and our desire to be in fellowship with him?

God is gracious, and he is always there for us when we are in a crisis. But a mature prayer life involves so much more than sending God our 911 calls and wish lists. Prayer involves so much more than saying, "Lord, gimme this," and "Lord, gimme that."

Many Christians today seem to have a weak and insipid walk with God. They lack power in their lives. They lack joy. They lack the ability to overcome sins and bad habits. Why do so many Christians experience such an anemic Christian life? I believe that, in most cases, it's because we fail to practice a biblical prayer life.

Paul is asking the Thessalonians to live a life of obedience to the Word of God and to pray for the power of God's Word to spread. That's what Jesus meant when he said, "Seek first—" Seek *what* first? Your needs? Your desires? Your wish list? Your dreams? No. "But seek first *his* kingdom and *his* righteousness, and all these things will be given to you as well" (Matthew 6:33).

I can testify that, over the years, as my prayer life has matured and become more focused on Jesus and his kingdom, I find myself hardly ever thinking about my own needs. My prayer life is a work in progress, and it is not what I want it to be, but I can see a process of maturity taking place the longer I seek God in prayer.

When our prayers become focused on our wants and desires instead of on the Father's glory, our prayer life becomes weak and ineffective. When we pray that God will give us wealth and possessions and a life of ease, there's a good chance we're not praying according to God's will.

God's priorities are reaching the lost and equipping the saints for ministry, not making sure that your house and car are the envy of the neighborhood. And when our selfish prayers go unanswered, what happens? Doubt sets in. We resent God for ignoring our immature and self-centered prayers. Our faith grows weak and our prayers lack confidence.

The reason Paul was confident that his prayers for the spread of the gospel would be answered was that such prayers are always consistent with God's will. Such prayers are always focused on God's glory. Such prayers are always prayed to lift up God's reputation, not ours.

Please understand, there's a difference between praying for yourself and praying selfishly. If you are sick, it's only natural and right to pray for healing. If you are in financial distress, it's only right to pray that God would meet your needs. If you are in prison for the sake of the gospel, it is understandable that you would pray to be released. Though Paul did pray for his physical needs, his prayers were overwhelmingly focused on the work of the ministry and the spread of the gospel. He prayed that souls would be saved and that God would be glorified.

OUR PRAYERS—AND SATAN'S SCHEMES

Some people have odd notions about prayer. They think that prayer is a matter of cajoling or manipulating God into doing what he doesn't want to do. They think that prayer is getting on God's good side and overcoming his reluctance to give them what they want. But these are not biblical views of God or of prayer.

Prayer is truly a two-way conversation with the Creator of the universe. It's not just talking to God but listening to him as well. When you study the prayer life of Jesus, when you look at the way he communed with God the Father, you realize that prayer ought to be as much a part of our lives as the air we breathe or the food we eat. Jesus, our role model for prayer, said, "My food is to do the will of him who sent me and to finish his work" (John 4:34). Until our communing with God is like air and food to us, we will not experience power and answered prayer.

Satan understands these truths far better than we do. He understands the power that believers receive from having a continual two-way communion with God. That's why he works overtime to distract us, to discourage us, to prevent us from building a habit of continual prayer. Satan does not want us to have that kind of intimacy with God, a kind of power that comes only from communing with God. So he does everything possible to disrupt our prayer life.

Once we become aware that Satan is working overtime to destroy our fellowship with God, a lot of problems begin to make sense. We recognize the opposition of Satan for what it is. We begin to understand why obstacles and problems crop up in our lives that discourage us from praying. We see why temptation and sin make us want to hide from God. We understand why times of ease and prosperity make us feel like we don't really need to spend time with God.

The Christian life is a spiritual battle. Our prayer life is under constant attack from the enemy, and the sooner we recognize these attacks, the more we will run to God in prayer, saying, "Lord, I need you! Shield me from temptation and deliver me from the enemy. I want to know the joy of continually resting in your presence."

Satan attacks us not only by trying to keep us from praying, but he also attacks us through other people. This is spiritual warfare. We need to remember that our real enemy is not flesh and blood. The people who attack us are dupes and stooges, doing Satan's bidding. Our real enemy is an invisible puppet-master who pulls the strings of godless people and makes them dance to his tune. But by giving themselves over to serve Satan's cause, they can do enormous harm to us as followers of Christ.

So Paul asks the Thessalonian believers to pray that God would protect him and his fellow workers from the attacks of godless men. He wrote: "And pray that we may be delivered from wicked and evil people, for not everyone has faith. But the Lord is faithful, and he will strengthen you and protect you from the evil one" (3:2-3).

Paul's concern is not primarily for his personal safety but that the advance of the gospel would not be hindered. We see the same attacks by evil people in our world today. A prime example is a phenomenon called "After School Satan Clubs." The first such club opened at an elementary school in Portland, Oregon, in September 2016. It was started by the Portland chapter of the Satanic Temple, a nationwide atheist organization headquartered in Salem, Massachusetts.

The organizers of the club say they do not believe in a literal, personal Satan, but that they use Satan as a symbol of "free thought." The group claims that the focus of the club is to promote "science and rational thinking" and encourage "benevolence and empathy for everybody." The satanically inspired group seeks to counteract the Good News Club sponsored by Child Evangelism Fellowship that meets after school. "Our goal, ultimately," the group's website proclaims, "is to place an [After School Satan Club] in every school where the Good News Clubs, or other proselytizing religious groups, have established a presence."[33]

It doesn't get any plainer than that. This is a direct satanic attack by evil people against the gospel of Jesus Christ. This is a group of people bent on halting the advance of the good news, and they plan to spread these Satan Clubs to other states.

Even though these atheists *think* they are merely promoting "science and rational thinking," even though they claim not to believe in a literal Satan, they are doing the bidding of the very devil they claim not to acknowledge. Satan himself must laugh at the irony: Here is an organization of self-styled rational thinkers, and they have founded a "temple" to glorify the name of Satan!

Paul's plea for intercession against the schemes of Satan is as urgent now as it was in his day. We should not be surprised at the venom and irrational hatred expressed by "rational" people against the good news of Jesus Christ. They are captives of Satan, and they are expressing the rage of their puppet-master. They accuse faithful evangelists and preachers of the gospel of being "haters." Why? Because authentic Christians refuse to sanction sin and immorality.

The gospel is called "good news" because it is a message of God's love for all humanity. It is a message of hope and salvation for those mired in self-destructive habits and lifestyles. The puppets of Satan who oppose the gospel want Christians to be accepting of sin, even though sin eats away at the body, soul, and spirit of those who practice it.

It's as if we called a cancer surgeon a "hater" because he refused to be accepting and tolerant of the malignant tumors in his patients. It's as if it's an act of "hate" for the surgeon to operate and remove the malignancy. Sin is a spiritual cancer, a moral malignancy, producing shame and self-destruction. Many forms of sin are physically destructive as well as morally destructive.

Jesus came to deliver the human race from sin and guilt. He died on the cross in order to absolve our sin with his own blood. The gospel is a message of 100 percent love. It does not contain an ounce, a molecule, or even a subatomic particle of hate. But leave it to Satan to turn logic upside-down, portraying good as evil—and love as hate.

Satan wants the world to believe that anyone who loves God and obeys his Word, anyone who refuses to accept sin and immorality, is a hater. He has twisted the truth into the vilest kind of lie. I once saw an atheist website that listed all the different kinds of people that Christians supposedly hate. As God is my witness, I can tell you with a pure conscience that I do not hate anyone in the world. I love everyone with the love of Jesus Christ. God is not willing that any should perish, and neither am I.

If you are a homosexual person, God loves you and so do I. If you are an atheist, God loves you and so do I. If you are a Muslim—even a radical Muslim who has sworn allegiance to ISIS—God loves you and so do I. If you have done horrible things in your life and you think you are beyond the reach of God's grace, God loves you and so do I. I have no hatred in my heart toward any person or any group or any race or any religion or toward anyone who is guilty of any sin.

I will not bless or condone what the Bible calls sin—not in my life nor in the life of any other human being. I will not call evil good. But I will not hate you. I will love you with the love of the Lord Jesus Christ, who gave himself for you and for me, who loved me and saved me from my sin.

OUR CONFIDENCE IN PRAYER

Let's take another look at verse 2: "And pray that we may be delivered from wicked and evil people, *for not everyone has faith*." I've italicized that last phrase because Paul is making an interesting and important point. Up to now, I have been talking about "wicked and evil people" in terms of atheists, secularists, Satanists, and others who vehemently oppose the gospel. But notice that Paul says "for not everyone has faith."

It's clear from that statement that Paul is talking about wicked and evil people who are *inside the church*. He is saying that much of the opposition that he and his partners in the ministry are facing actually comes from people *in the church* who pose as Christians, but who are actually infiltrators and false teachers. They claim to be Christians, but they do not have faith.

Such people are among us in the church today. They may be leaders in the church. They may even preach from the pulpit. But they don't believe the truth of the gospel. They are hostile to the good news and to those who faithfully preach it. They attack those who preach that Jesus is the only way to salvation. They intimidate those who uphold the authority of the Word of God.

Tragically, many pastors who believe the gospel lack the strength and the character to stand up to the wicked and evil people who have infiltrated the church. These cowed and intimidated pastors may tell themselves they are trying to keep the peace within the church, but by their weakness, they are simply appeasing and surrendering to those who oppose the truth.

When we find we are being attacked for standing firm for the gospel, we need to remember Paul's promise in verse 3: "But the Lord is faithful, and he will strengthen you and protect you from the evil one." We must not hate those who oppose us in the church—but we should not yield one inch of God's truth. We should always seek to love everyone in the church and to live peaceably with other members of the body of Christ. But when God's truth comes under attack, we must ask God to strengthen us and protect us as we go head-to-head with the evil one.

In verse 4, Paul tells us, "We have confidence in the Lord that you are doing and will continue to do the things we command." So, as we pray, let us pray with confidence in the Lord.

We are confident that God is faithful to keep all his promises. He is faithful to strengthen us—he will not allow us to be tempted beyond our ability to bear. God is faithful to provide a way of escape. God is faithful to his Word—it will not return to him empty. God is faithful to give strength when strength is needed. He is faithful to keep Satan from tormenting his children. God is faithful to shield us from the spirit of lawlessness. He is faithful to keep us from stumbling. God is faithful to keep us blameless with great joy.

That is our confidence. Our confidence is not founded on our brilliant strategy. It's not founded on our clever marketing techniques. It's not founded on our own labor. Our confidence is in the Lord alone, that he will enable us to do the work he has called us to do.

Finally, in verse 5, Paul says, "May the Lord direct your hearts into God's love and Christ's perseverance." The love of God motivates everything we do. And the example that Christ set for us enables us to persevere through hardships and opposition. Paul has confidence that God, who began a great work in the lives of the Thessalonian believers, will carry it through to completion. And we have that same confidence in God today.

John Wanamaker (1838–1922) was a wealthy American merchant, a pioneer in the field of advertising and marketing, and a US postmaster general. Any of these occupations would have been career enough for one man, yet John Wanamaker considered them all sidelines compared to his true calling and career. What was that calling and career? I'll tell you in a moment.

He opened his first business, a Philadelphia department store called Oak Hall, in 1861. He revolutionized the mercantile trade by putting price tags on all his goods; until Wanamaker came along, merchants dickered with customers over the price, so that different customers paid different prices based on their bargaining ability. Wanamaker also pioneered the notion of making merchandise returnable, and earned the title "the Merchant Prince."

In 1875, Wanamaker purchased an abandoned railroad depot in Philadelphia and converted it into a large shopping mall called the Depot, with 129 separate stores under one roof. He soon expanded, opening stores in New York City, London, and Paris. In 1889, he founded First Penny Savings Bank to encourage people to save for the future. That same year, he was appointed postmaster general by President Benjamin Harrison. He also founded numerous charities, including a rescue mission, a homeless shelter, and a free school for mechanical trades. He donated the funds to build the children's wing of Philadelphia's Presbyterian Hospital.

A devout Christian, Wanamaker refused to open his stores or advertise on Sundays. In his Philadelphia store, he had one soundproof room that he used for a single purpose: prayer. Every day, he spent a minimum of a half-hour reading God's Word and praying. He eagerly shared the good news of Jesus Christ with everyone he met. He said, "If you once have the joy and sweet pleasure of bringing one soul to Christ, you will be hungry to get another."

Now, I'll tell you what he considered his true calling: John Wanamaker was the superintendent of the Sunday school at Bethany Presbyterian Church—the largest Sunday school in the world at that time. He was once asked how he had time to be in charge of such a large Sunday school when he had so many businesses to run.

Wanamaker replied that the Sunday school was his first priority—everything else he was involved in was secondary. He explained, "Early in life I read, 'Seek ye first the kingdom of God, and his righteousness, and all these things shall be added unto you.' The Sunday school is my business; all the rest are the things."[34]

God will honor the prayers of his faithful and obedient followers. But in order to honor those prayers, we have to be on our knees *praying* those prayers. Do you have a biblical prayer life? Do you daily have a two-way conversation with God?

15

THE GIFT OF WORK

2 Thessalonians 3:6-18

The so-called "Occupy Movement" began in September 2011 with the "Occupy Wall Street" protest in New York City's Zuccotti Park. Within a month, Occupy protests had spread to nearly a thousand cities in more than eighty nations, including six hundred cities across the United States. Protesters claimed to represent the "99 percent" (the common people) against the "1 percenters," the privileged few who profited outrageously from the global financial system.

Now, I don't defend Wall Street or the worldly financial system. It was greed in the banking system and on Wall Street, combined with foolish and corrupt government policies, that produced the economic meltdown of 2008. So the Occupy protesters were largely correct in their diagnosis of a major social, political, and economic problem in the world. But they could not have been more wrong-headed in their prescription to heal that problem.

The Occupy people were largely anarchists, socialists, and Communists, and their solution was to take all the wealth away from wealthy people and redistribute it to everyone else—especially to people who were unwilling to work and earn a living for themselves and their families.

That word *occupy* reminds me of the words of Jesus from a parable he told in Luke 19, shortly before his crucifixion. It's the story of a nobleman who was going away on a trip (symbolizing the Lord Jesus himself, who is about to die, rise again, and ascend to heaven). The nobleman gathered ten of his servants, entrusted a sum of money to each one, and told them, "Put this money to work until I come back" (Luke 19:13). The King James Version uses an interesting turn of phrase for this command: "Occupy till I come."

No, those two translations do not contradict each other. The King James Version of 1611 uses *occupy* to mean "be busy," or "work hard," or "use your time productively." This nobleman, who symbolizes Jesus, was telling his servants, "Don't be lazy. Don't just sit around all day. Use your time wisely. Invest this money wisely. Make sure you keep yourself—and my money—occupied in a profitable way while I'm gone."

This is a far cry from the way the Occupy protesters used the word. To them, to occupy a park was to pitch a tent and sit around all day, pounding drums and smoking weed and pretending to make some sort of important statement. It also meant destroying the beauty of the park with trash and human waste, and leaving that mess for other people to clean up. Their use of *occupy* is the exact opposite of the way Jesus used that word in his parable.

A lot of people, out of either ignorance or dishonesty, have tried to portray Jesus as a socialist. But how does Jesus portray himself in this parable? He uses the analogy of a nobleman, an employer, a businessman, a capitalist—the kind of person the Occupy protesters would call a "1 percenter." Now, I'm not saying that Jesus was a capitalist—this parable is all about making *spiritual* investments and reaping *spiritual* rewards. But it's equally clear that Jesus is not condemning those who make a profit through hard work and putting capital at risk. He is saying that it is a good thing for people to be occupied with the honorable labor of making a living. Jesus is, in essence, telling a parable about free-market economics to make a point of eternal spiritual significance.

Those who participated in the Occupy Movement have very little understanding of how economies work, how wealth is created, and how America became so economically powerful. Many were undoubtedly brainwashed by Marxist university professors. They blamed America for all the oppression and injustice in the world, ignoring the fact that America has done more to overthrow oppression and eliminate injustice than any other nation in history.

Though it's undeniable that American history is stained by the legacy of slavery, the mistreatment of Native Americans, interference in the affairs of other sovereign nations, and so forth, these events do not *reflect* American principles. Rather, they are *violations* of our cherished principles. Justice and liberty are always the result of *living up to the principles* of America's founding documents, the Declaration of Independence and the United States Constitution.

THE PROTESTANT WORK ETHIC

One of the fundamental ethical principles that has always defined America as a nation and as a people is the Protestant work ethic. According to this ethical principle, if we practice the values of hard work, self-discipline, and frugality that are affirmed in God's Word, we will prosper, provide for our own families, and still have enough to support God's work and to meet the needs of the less fortunate.

The Protestant work ethic promotes personal responsibility. We cannot simply sit in a tent in the park, beating a drum and feeling entitled to other people's money. The world does not owe us a living for simply existing. While we have great compassion for the poor and needy, able-bodied people who refuse to work have no legitimate claim on the earnings of hard-working people. That's not my opinion. That's the clear declaration of the Word of God.

The act of taking away the hard-earned resources of American citizens by the force of law and squandering it on subsidies for the lazy is contrary to the Scriptures. Socialism is unbiblical, unchristian, and unworkable. It destroys incentive, destroys the economy, and destroys human dignity. I lived for fifteen years under a socialist system in Egypt. I saw the leaders of the government taking wealth from productive people and using it to empower themselves and their political cronies. I saw greed and political corruption strangle the economy of Egypt, until a nation that was once the breadbasket of the region become a basket case.

At this point you may be getting a little uncomfortable. You might be thinking, *I didn't expect this to be a political book. I thought this was a book about fearless living in troubled times.* But I'm not talking about politics. I'm not telling you which party to support or which candidates to vote for. I have talked only about biblical principles. God calls us to live out the Christian faith according to certain principles from his Word—principles concerning worship, witnessing, giving, and how we live our lives.

But there is a problem in the way people often preach and teach about the Christian life. Many Christians have developed a pietistic view of the faith, the notion that the Christian faith only relates to our individual spirituality and holiness—not how we conduct ourselves out in the world. It's as if we worship a Sunday-only God, and the rest of the week we are free to live as secularists.

Our faith impacts every aspect of our lives, from our Sunday worship to our Monday work, from our piety to our politics. No aspect of our lives is outside the purview and authority of Scripture. Here in the third and final chapter of 2 Thessalonians, Paul shows us that even our work ethic and our social theory are subordinate to the authority of Scripture. Paul goes so far as to say that there are limits to what we commonly refer to as "compassion" or "charity." Those who are able to work but refuse to do so should not be coddled and enabled. They should not be fed. They should be ostracized. He writes:

In the name of the Lord Jesus Christ, we command you, brothers and sisters, to keep away from every believer who is idle and disruptive and does not live according to the teaching you received from us. For you yourselves know how you ought to follow our example. We were not idle when we were with you, nor did we eat anyone's food without paying for it. On the contrary, we worked night and day, laboring and toiling so that we would not be a burden to any of you. We did this, not because we do not have the right to such help, but in order to offer ourselves as a model for you to imitate. For even when we were with you, we gave you this rule: "The one who is unwilling to work shall not eat."

We hear that some among you are idle and disruptive. They

are not busy; they are busybodies. Such people we command and urge in the Lord Jesus Christ to settle down and earn the food they eat. And as for you, brothers and sisters, never tire of doing what is good.

Take special note of anyone who does not obey our instruction in this letter. Do not associate with them, in order that they may feel ashamed. Yet do not regard them as an enemy, but warn them as you would a fellow believer (2 Thessalonians 3:6-15).

Many people see work as a necessary evil. This view is expressed in the bumper sticker that says, "I owe, I owe, so off to work I go." Many Christians have the mistaken belief that work is a curse, a consequence of the fall. But a careful reading of Genesis shows this is not so. In Genesis 2, we read, "The LORD God took the man and put him in the Garden of Eden to work it and take care of it" (Genesis 2:15). God gave Adam, a man who had committed no sin, work to do in the Garden of Eden. Working in a garden is honorable, healthy, and pleasurable, as any weekend gardener will tell you.

But after Adam and Eve sinned, something changed, as God explains in the next chapter of Genesis:

> To Adam he said, "Because you listened to your wife and ate fruit from the tree about which I commanded you, 'You must not eat from it,'
>
> > "Cursed is the ground because of you;
> >   through painful toil you will eat food from it
> >   all the days of your life.
> > It will produce thorns and thistles for you,
> >   and you will eat the plants of the field.
> > By the sweat of your brow
> >   you will eat your food
> > until you return to the ground,
> >   since from it you were taken;
> > for dust you are
> >   and to dust you will return" (Genesis 3:17-19).

Work is not a curse from God: work is a blessing. I'm confident that the redeemed race of Adam will have plenty of work to do in heaven, in the New Jerusalem.

THE IDLE AND DISRUPTIVE

The curse of sin was inflicted on the ground itself. Adam and Eve were cast out of the Garden of Eden, where tending the garden had been a pleasant and joyful experience. In order to coax food from the ground, they would now have to contend with thorns and thistles that try to choke the healthy plants. They would have to compete with pests and plant diseases and fruit-stealing animals. Food that was once plentiful in the garden paradise would become subject to drought and blight and catastrophic weather.

Work is not a curse, but the conditions under which Adam and Eve would work for their food had been cursed. The once-enjoyable task of gardening became a sweaty, stinking chore, filled with anxiety and uncertainty. Some years, there would be months of work with nothing to show for it but crop failure and heartbreak.

In spite of the fall, work is still a blessing. Whenever an honest day's work is exchanged for an honest day's pay, that work is honoring to God. We should never dishonor what God calls good, and God says that honest work is a good thing, one of the blessings of his creation.

When the Christian faith burst upon the scene in the Roman-dominated culture of the first century, followers of Christ elevated the status of honest work to a level unknown in the Greco-Roman world. Upper-class Greeks and Romans viewed labor, especially physical labor, as beneath their dignity. By contrast, the Bible teaches from cover to cover that hard work, productivity, investment, ownership, job creation, wealth creation, profit, and prosperity are all honorable and consistent with the righteousness of the Lord.

God created human beings with an instinctive desire to be creative, productive, industrious, and innovative. He created us with an instinctive ambition to acquire property to own and exploit for the good of ourselves and our families. God created us with an instinctive urge to create products and wealth, and he ordained that the firstfruits of our labors would be dedicated to him as an act of gratitude and worship.

When we work, we imitate God and bring glory to God. The Scriptures tell us that God labored for six days, then rested on the seventh, which is the same pattern of labor that most of us follow to this day. Why does our imitation of God give glory to him? Because when we are industrious, creative, and productive, we reflect the character of God in our lives.

Those who are able to work but refuse to work are not only dishonoring to themselves—they are dishonoring to God. That's why people who claim to be Christians and support the Occupy movement, those who want to dismantle the free-market system and replace it with a socialist system of wealth redistribution, are not biblical Christians. I'm not questioning whether they are truly saved. But I do question their discernment and their understanding of the Scriptures.

If anyone claims (as many defenders of the "social gospel" do) that God wants us to tax work and productivity while subsidizing indolence and dependence, I have to ask: Where do you find that in the Scriptures? Paul says quite clearly that we are to "keep away from every believer who is idle and disruptive and does not live according to the teaching you received from us…For even when we were with you, we gave you this rule: 'The one who is unwilling to work shall not eat.'" Invoking the authority of Jesus himself, Paul said that those who are "idle and disruptive" must "settle down and earn the food they eat."

There is a simple principle we should always remember: What you tax, you get less of; what you subsidize, you get more of. If you tax work and productivity, you are punishing work and productivity, and you will get less of it. If you subsidize laziness and a dependent attitude, you will get more laziness, more dependence, and you will destroy the God-given, God-like, God-honoring industriousness that was stamped into our being as part of God's own image.

When we discourage work, when we tolerate and encourage laziness, we denigrate humanity and dishonor the image of God within us. Genesis 1:31 says that "God saw all that he had made, and it was very good." He was pleased with his handiwork, the fruit of his labor.

As the Landlord of Creation, God delighted in his ownership of the created universe.

Yet all too often, people who claim to speak for God have tried to erase that aspect of God's image from human nature. They have tried to destroy our God-like love of work, our God-like love of ownership, our God-like eagerness to be productive and provide for our families. The social engineers with their "social gospel" may or may not have the best of intentions (many, I suspect, are merely inflating their own egos and social standing by attempting to appear more compassionate, enlightened, and progressive than other people)—but even if we impute good intentions to them, we should never forget what the road to hell is paved with!

God created a natural order that rewards creativity and industriousness and punishes laziness. It is the height of folly to try to upend God's natural order and try to invert God's system of punishments and rewards. Paul said, "Follow God's example, therefore, as dearly loved children" (Ephesians 5:1). When we imitate God's excellent qualities, we bring joy to his heart—the joy a loving father experiences when he sees his little children walking in his footsteps.

A BIBLICAL VIEW OF WORK

How do we glorify God in the workplace? By taking ownership of our work. I'm not saying you have to be a business owner to glorify God. Even as an employee, you can take ownership of your work and glorify God in the process. What does it mean to "take ownership" of the work you do?

First, whether you are an employer or an employee, you take ownership when you do every task with a desire to please your ultimate employer, God himself. As Paul said, "Whatever you do, work at it with all your heart, as working for the Lord, not for human masters" (Colossians 3:23). Do more than you have to, work harder than you're required to, deliver more quality and excellence than people expect. Why? Because you're ultimately working for the Lord.

Second, you take ownership when you do everything with absolute integrity and honesty. God said, "You shall not steal," so never take ethical shortcuts. Nobody steals from himself, right? So when you take ownership of your work, you maintain absolute honesty as if you are working solely for yourself. If you are an employer, you deal fairly and squarely with your employees and your customers. If you are an employee, you treat the boss's property, time, money, and customers as if they were your own.

Third, you take ownership when you look at your work from God's perspective. We see this principle clearly in the Old Testament book of Ecclesiastes, written by King Solomon. There, Solomon calls himself "the Teacher." He begins writing from the perspective of someone who is self-centered, who is unable to see his work from God's perspective. As a result, he denigrates his work as an act of futility:

> "Meaningless! Meaningless!"
> says the Teacher.
> "Utterly meaningless!
> Everything is meaningless."
> What do people gain from all their labors
> at which they toil under the sun?…
> My heart took delight in all my labor,
> and this was the reward for all my toil.
> Yet when I surveyed all that my hands had done
> and what I had toiled to achieve,
> everything was meaningless, a chasing after the wind;
> nothing was gained under the sun.
> (Ecclesiastes 1:2-3; 2:10b-11)

Later, Solomon describes his attitude when he is able to see his labor from God's perspective. He wrote:

> What do workers gain from their toil?…I know that there is nothing better for people than to be happy and to do good while they live. That each of them may eat and drink, and find satisfaction in all their toil—this is the gift of God (Ecclesiastes 3:9,12-13).

Work brings satisfaction, and that satisfaction is a gift from God. As we learn to appreciate the ability to work, and as we treasure our work as a gift from God, we take ownership of it, and our work becomes what God intended work to be—a source of provision, a source of wealth creation, a source of satisfaction, and a means of giving back to God and showing compassion to others. Even if you think the work you do is drudgery, even if your tasks are unpleasant and the people you work with are unhelpful and unfriendly, your work can still be glorifying to God and satisfying for you—if you view your work from God's perspective.

Work is not a curse; it's a gift from God. When we understand the work we do from a biblical perspective, it ceases to be drudgery. It becomes a golden opportunity to glorify God. By placing the work we do in a biblical context, by understanding that we don't work primarily for the boss or the company or the customer but for God, we can better understand the words of Paul in 2 Thessalonians 3:10—"For even when we were with you, we gave you this rule: 'The one who is unwilling to work shall not eat.'"

Does that sound harsh and unloving to you? Actually, this approach is the height of authentic love. It's an approach called "tough love." Sometimes the worst thing you can do for people is to shower them with compassion, to meet all their needs and solve all their problems. And sometimes the best thing you can do for people is to withhold charity, to say no to their pleas for help, and to say, "You created this situation, and you need to solve this problem yourself. Experience is a teacher, and you need to learn the lessons of this experience."

When Paul gave advice to a church in his letters, he always addressed a real and urgent problem in that church. There were lazy, unproductive people in the church in Thessalonica. They were freeloading off the industrious, hard-working people in that church—and the Christians in Thessalonica were letting these parasites get away with it. Paul doesn't tell us *why* the Thessalonian Christians were putting up with these freeloaders. But the fact that Paul has to give this advice to the church suggests a parallel with our own culture today. We keep hearing that there are "jobs that Americans won't do." This is a recent phenomenon. In prior generations—and especially during the Great Depression—there were *no* jobs Americans wouldn't do to keep body and soul together.

Apparently, there were people in the Thessalonian church who would rather accept a handout than get their hands dirty. If you suggested they go out and look for work, they would smugly reply, "There are some jobs that Thessalonians won't do!" Paul doesn't discuss the motives of these unproductive Thessalonians. He doesn't tell us if they were simply lazy or if they were so sure of Christ's imminent return that they saw no need to work. Their reasons don't matter. Idleness is a sin, and this sin needed to be confronted, not enabled.

HOW TO MOTIVATE THE UNMOTIVATED

In this passage, Paul suggests six incentives to help motivate and energize those who engage in the sin of idleness. He suggests a six-point plan for getting these unproductive Thessalonians back into the workforce where they belong.

1. *Ostracize them.* The first of Paul's six incentives is to ostracize the idle person. It's important to notice that Paul does not give the Thessalonians a suggestion about idle people. He does not give them an option. He gives them a *command*—not on his own apostolic authority but by the highest authority of all, the authority of the Lord Jesus himself. He says, "In the name of the Lord Jesus Christ, we command you, brothers and sisters, to keep away from every believer who is idle and disruptive and does not live according to the teaching you received from us" (3:6).

They should be disfellowshipped, avoided, shunned. They should be taught that such self-centered, sinful behavior is not tolerated in the church. Many in the church tend to be soft-hearted and indulgent toward those who engage in a pattern of sin. We don't like to confront. We don't like to make people feel uncomfortable. We don't want them to be upset with us.

The notion of church discipline has become a touchy subject these days, something we rarely speak about. This is partly because, in some churches, discipline has been misused and abused. But biblical discipline is good for the health of a church. The Lord Jesus instituted a four-step process of discipline so that his church could be protected from predators and evildoers. Jesus said:

> "If your brother or sister sins, go and point out their fault, just between the two of you. If they listen to you, you have won them over. But if they will not listen, take one or two others along, so that 'every matter may be established by the testimony of two or three witnesses.' If they still refuse to listen, tell it to the church; and if they refuse to listen even to the church, treat them as you would a pagan or a tax collector" (Matthew 18:15-17).

Jesus outlines four steps in this passage. First, if you become aware that one of your fellow Christians is sinning, you go privately to that person and discuss the matter with him or her in the hopes that this person will respond and repent. But if that person will not listen, then take the matter to the next level.

Second, you take one or two other witnesses along to establish a record of testimony about this matter. The matter is still being dealt with privately, without bringing any undue embarrassment upon the one who has sinned. But if the sinning person still will not listen, then you must take the matter to the next higher level.

Third, what was a private and closely guarded matter now *must* become public. You *must* tell it to the church. Will the sinning person listen to the entire church? If not, then you must take the matter to the next and final level.

Fourth, you (and the church) treat this person as you would an unbeliever, an outcast. You must ostracize this person and put him or her out of your fellowship.

Paul is saying that such people are out of line, living contrary to the Scriptures, and creating disorder in the body of Christ. That is why the idle and disruptive person cannot be tolerated. He must either repent and change his behavior—or he must be removed from fellowship.

The goal of church discipline is repentance and redemption, not permanent rejection. If the sinning individual sincerely repents, we gladly welcome him or her back into the fellowship of believers.

2. *Paul's own example.* The second incentive Paul offers is his own example of hard work. He writes, "For you yourselves know how you ought to follow our example. We were not idle when we were with you, nor did we eat anyone's food without paying for it. On the contrary, we worked night and day, laboring and toiling so that we would not be a burden to any of you" (3:7-8). Paul set a good example as a Christian who worked hard and earned his keep. Those who refuse to work place an unfair burden on their brothers and sisters in the church. Paul showed the Thessalonians how an authentic Christian is supposed to live.

There is no point in preaching a strong work ethic to my children or my congregation if I am not practicing what I preach. When we set a good example, we serve as an inspirational, motivational role model for others. A consistent example communicates more effectively than a thousand sermons. Paul could confidently point to himself as a role model because his example of hard work had been witnessed by the entire church. He practiced what he preached.

3. *Hunger.* An empty belly is a great motivator—perhaps the best motivator of all. Paul said, "The one who is unwilling to work shall not eat." Those words should be posted in every government office from Washington, DC, to the smallest villages and hamlets. Our government should encourage industriousness and self-reliance. Instead, government punishes industriousness and encourages dependence. The US government, under President Lyndon Johnson, declared war on poverty in 1964. It's a war we've been losing ever since—largely because the welfare state has been *subsidizing and incentivizing* poverty. A 2012 analysis by the highly respected Cato Institute concluded:

> News that the poverty rate has risen to 15.1 percent of Americans, the highest level in nearly a decade, has set off a predictable round of calls for increased government spending on social welfare programs. Yet this year the federal government will spend more than $668 billion on at least 126 different programs to fight poverty. And that does not even begin to count welfare spending by state and local governments, which adds $284 billion to that figure. In total, the

United States spends nearly $1 trillion every year to fight poverty. That amounts to $20,610 for every poor person in America, or $61,830 per poor family of three.

Welfare spending increased significantly under President George W. Bush and has exploded under President Barack Obama. In fact, since President Obama took office, federal welfare spending has increased by 41 percent, more than $193 billion per year. Despite this government largess, more than 46 million Americans continue to live in poverty. Despite nearly $15 trillion in total welfare spending since Lyndon Johnson declared war on poverty in 1964, the poverty rate is perilously close to where we began more than 40 years ago.[35]

In his autobiography, Ronald Reagan told a story from his early life that helped shape his views on the welfare state. When Ronald was a college student during the Great Depression, his father, Jack, worked as an administrator of federal relief programs in Dixon, Illinois. Every week, people who were out of work would come to Jack Reagan's office to pick up food and coupons they could exchange for groceries. Young Ronald would sometimes visit his father at the office. He recalled:

> I was shocked to see the fathers of many of my schoolmates waiting in line for handouts...Jack knew that accepting handouts was tough on the dignity of the men and came up with a plan to help them recover some of it. He began leaving home early in the morning and making rounds of the county, asking if anyone had odd jobs available...When the men came in for their handouts, Jack offered the work he'd found to those who'd been out of work the longest.

> I'll never forget the faces of these men when Jack told them their turn had come up for a job...I swear the men were standing a little taller. They wanted *work*, not handouts.

> Not long after that, Jack told several men he had found a week's work for them. They responded to this news with a

rustling of feet. Eventually, one broke the silence and said: "Jack, the last time you got me some work, the people at the relief office took my family off welfare; they said I had a job and even though it was temporary, I wasn't eligible for relief anymore. I just can't afford to take another job."[36]

What you subsidize, you get more of; what you penalize, you get less of. The government bureaucracy always subsidizes idleness while penalizing work. The government always subsidizes poverty and dependence while penalizing initiative and self-reliance. If you want to understand why we spend $1 trillion a year fighting a losing "war on poverty," there's your answer, as plain as it can be.

As I write these words, America has spent itself nearly $20 trillion into debt, with a large portion of that money going to pay able-bodied people not to work. Like Paul, I'm 100 percent in favor of helping those who are truly needy—widows, orphans, the aged, and the mentally or physically disabled. The welfare system was originally created as a safety net for the truly needy. In all too many cases, however, it has become a hammock for the truly lazy.

Most of the problems in our society could be better solved by private charities and the church than by a wasteful government bureaucracy. The war on poverty is not the government's responsibility. It's the church's responsibility to meet these needs.

You might say, "But the church can't afford to spend $1 trillion per year to shelter the poor and feed the hungry." But the church wouldn't need to spend $1 trillion per year. Those who are truly incapable of supporting themselves and their families are a tiny fraction of the people who are now dependent on the government. American taxpayers pay out such huge sums of money (and the government goes deeper into debt every year) because we pay perfectly able, healthy people *not* to work. We subsidize poverty.

If the church were in charge of caring for the poor, the poor would be cared for—and those who are capable of working would work or they would not eat. Anyone who thinks that is mean or hard-hearted has his thinking cap on backward. It is *compassionate* to teach people to be responsible and self-reliant. By subsidizing poverty, we subsidize all sorts of social ills—crime, the neglect and abuse of children, drug abuse, abortion, and on and on.

True compassion can be exercised only by following the biblical principles in 2 Thessalonians 3:6-18. Subsidizing poverty may make you *feel* warm and fuzzy. You may pat yourself on the back for your self-styled compassion. But all you've done is contribute to the destruction of lives, the destruction of human character, and the destruction of society. Let's obey God's Word and start encouraging the work ethic once more.

4. *Harmony in the church.* Paul wrote, "We hear that some among you are idle and disruptive. They are not busy; they are busybodies. Such people we command and urge in the Lord Jesus Christ to settle down and earn the food they eat" (3:11-12). Paul draws an interesting contrast here between people who are *busy* and people who are *busybodies*. People who are busy working don't have time to be disruptive and divisive. Lazy people seem to have all the time in the world to go about sowing dissension, spreading gossip, and making a nuisance of themselves. For the sake of harmony in the body of Christ, idle people should be required to work.

Another way deadbeats and freeloaders bring disharmony into the church is by making it difficult for hard-working believers to distinguish between those who are truly in need and those who are not. We are called by God to help the genuinely needy and to give generously to those who cannot care for themselves. Idle people waste the resources that others have sacrificially donated to help the genuinely poor.

When a hard-working believer gives sacrificially to help the poor, and then sees his donation go to some lazy layabout who refuses to help himself, he becomes jaded and cynical. He thinks, "I'm willing to work hard and sacrifice some of my income to help people in need. But when I see my donations going to support lazy people, I have to wonder why I'm working so hard and why am I giving so much, only to see it all wasted. That's it! I'm through being taken advantage of. I'm not donating one more dime to support a lazy lifestyle."

We in the church care for the needy in the name of the Lord. And in the name of the same Lord, for the sake of harmony in the church, Paul commands us: "The one who is unwilling to work shall not eat."

5. *Shame.* Paul wrote, "Take special note of anyone who does not obey our instruction in this letter. Do not associate with them, *in order that they may feel ashamed*" (3:14). In our culture today, shame has a bad reputation—and with some good reason. It's tragic when children or adults become emotionally paralyzed due to toxic shame, especially shame they don't deserve, shame that was inflicted on them by an abuser.

But the capacity to feel shame *over sin* is a good thing. When Adam and Eve sinned, they realized they were naked—and they were ashamed. They tried to cover their nakedness, and they hid themselves from the searching gaze of a holy God. That is a healthy shame response to sin. It shows they had a conscience. I can testify personally to the power of shame as a positive motivator.

When I was a rebellious teenager, my family was well known in the community for faith and godliness. Whenever I got in trouble, one of the first things my parents reminded me of was that I had brought shame on the family name. During my rebellious years, there were not many things my parents could tell me that would make a difference in my behavior—but the appeal to shame almost always worked, at least for a while. I did not want to cause shame to my family, and I did not want to feel ashamed myself.

It is this healthy capacity for shame that we in the church need to tap into whenever fellow believers sin and need to be corrected. The purpose of shame is to prompt us to repentance.

6. *Love.* The final motivation Paul suggests is the motivation of love. He writes, "Yet do not regard them as an enemy, but warn them as you would a fellow believer" (3:15). Even when you ostracize the unproductive person, even when you cut off fellowship with that person, you don't do so out of hatred—you do so out of love. This is "tough love" in action. Our goal is to restore that person to fellowship in the body of Christ—not drive that person out of the body. Love must always be our goal.

Galatians 6:1 tells us, "Brothers and sisters, if someone is caught in a sin, you who live by the Spirit should restore that person gently. But watch yourselves, or you also may be tempted." Restore that person gently, not angrily. Not resentfully. Not vengefully. We are to restore that person as lovingly as possible, knowing that we ourselves may need to be corrected one day.

GRACE AND PEACE

Paul concludes with a prayer for those believers in Thessalonica—and for all believers, in all times, in all places:

> Now may the Lord of peace himself give you peace at all times and in every way. The Lord be with all of you.
>
> I, Paul, write this greeting in my own hand, which is the distinguishing mark in all my letters. This is how I write.
>
> The grace of our Lord Jesus Christ be with you all (2 Thessalonians 3:16-18).

Paul closes with a benediction of peace, and he adds this benediction in his own handwriting (Paul dictated most, if not all, of his letters to an *amanuensis* or secretary). The church, which had been misled in the past by false letters from false teachers, now had a sample of Paul's own handwriting. If any future letter came purporting to be from Paul, they would be able to authenticate it by the distinguishing mark of Paul's handwriting.

In his benediction, Paul prays that the Lord of peace would grant them peace in all circumstances and that he would bless them with his presence. Paul's prayer echoes down through the ages and continues to bless our lives today in the twenty-first century.

We live in troubled times—but we need not fear the days to come. As history moves toward a dramatic conclusion, as we await the revelation of our Lord Jesus Christ, as we anticipate the final stage of our redemption, the Lord of peace continues to answer Paul's closing prayer. The Lord of history continues to grant us his peace in these troubled times.

Terrorism, economic trouble, racial violence, social disorder, natural disaster, wars and rumors of war—all of these things will come. Let not your heart be troubled. God is never caught by surprise. God is never worried or anxious. God is never unsure or stressed. God is never threatened or intimidated. God is always at peace, in perfect harmony with himself. And his peace is our peace.

We serve the Lord of peace, and he is with us at all times. The God of grace found us in our sin, reached down to us in our sin, and saved us from our sin. He will sustain us as he leads us to heaven to be forever with him.

Never fear. The grace and peace of the Lord Jesus shall be with you, now and forevermore.

Notes

1. Will Hutton, "Only Fundamental Social Change Can Defeat the Anxiety Epidemic," *The Guardian*, May 7, 2016, www.theguardian.com/global/commentisfree/2016/may/07/mental-health-policy -anxiety-natasha-devon-young-people.

2. Tom Bartlett, "A Year After the Non-Apocalypse: Where Are They Now?," *Religion Dispatches* (USC Annenberg), May 21, 2012, http://religiondispatches.org/a-year-after-the-non-apocalypse -where-are-they-now/.

3. Quentin Cooper, "Our Never Ending Obsession with the Apocalypse," *BBC*, November 18, 2014, www.bbc.com/future/story/20121205-our-endless-apocalypse-obsession.

4. J. Barton Payne, *Encyclopedia of Biblical Prophecy: The Complete Guide to Scriptural Predictions and Their Fulfillment* (Grand Rapids: Baker, 1973), 13, 674-75.

5. Craig Unger, "American Rapture," *Vanity Fair* (Hive section), December 2005, www.vanityfair .com/news/2005/12/rapture200512.

6. C.S. Lewis, *Mere Christianity* (New York: HarperCollins, 1952, 2001), 134.

7. "The Second Coming of Jesus," *Pew Research Center*, April 21, 2009, www.pewresearch.org/ daily-number/the-second-coming-of-jesus/.

8. Charles M. Sell, *Unfinished Business: Helping Adult Children Resolve Their Past* (Portland, OR: Multnomah, 1989), 171-72.

9. A.W. Tozer, *The Next Chapter After the Last: For the Child of God, the Best Is Yet to Come* (Camp Hill, PA: WingSpread Publications, 2010), Kindle edition.

10. Jennifer Senior, "In Conversation: Antonin Scalia," *New York Magazine*, October 6, 2013, http:// nymag.com/news/features/antonin-scalia-2013-10/index3.html.

11. C.S. Lewis, *The Screwtape Letters* (New York: HarperCollins, 1942, 1996), ix.

12. Martin H. Manser, *The Westminster Collection of Christian Quotations* (Louisville, KY: Westminster John Knox Press, 2001), 72.

13. Dennis Prager, "Judaism's Sexual Revolution: Why Judaism (and then Christianity) Rejected Homosexuality," *Crisis Magazine*, September 1993, www.orthodoxytoday.org/articles2/Prager Homosexuality.php.

14. Ibid.

15. Ibid.

16. Robert L. Evans, *The Jew in the Plan of God* (Neptune, NJ: Loizeaux Brothers, 1950), 148-52. Quoted text altered slightly for clarity.

17. Fanny Crosby (lyrics) and William Howard Doane (melody), "To God Be the Glory," first published in 1875 (public domain).

18. Henry C. McCook, *The Gospel in Nature* (Philadelphia: Allen, Lane and Scott, 1887), 95-96.

19. Charles Colson with Ellen Santilli Vaughn, "Welcome to McChurch," *Christianity Today*, November 23, 1992, www.rebuildjournal.org/articles/mcchurch.html.

20. Victor Hugo, *Ninety-Three (Quatrevingt-Treize)*, trans. Mrs. Aline Delano (Boston: Little, Brown, and Company, 1889), www.gutenberg.org/files/49372/49372-h/49372-h.htm.

21. Henry W. Frost, "Uncommon Christians," China Inland Mission, 1914, Cornell University Library's Wason Pamphlet Collection (vol. 91, pamphlet 21), https://ecommons.cornell.edu/

bitstream/handle/1813/29894/Z191_21_0807.pdf;jsessionid=40D4C7DCAF7811CD20870A
BC61911319?sequence=1.

22. David Egner, "Try Thanksgiving," *Our Daily Bread*, November 22, 2000, http://odb.org/2000/11/22/try-thanksgiving/.

23. Fiona Ross, *Dining with the Rich and Royal* (Lanham, MD: Rowman and Littlefield, 2016), 204.

24. The King James Version of 1611 refers to the Holy Spirit as "it" in several places, such as 1 Peter 1:11, which says of the Holy Spirit, "it testified beforehand the sufferings of Christ, and the glory that should follow." The vast majority of New Testament scholars acknowledge this to be a mistranslation. The New International Version correctly renders this passage, "he predicted the sufferings of the Messiah and the glories that would follow."

25. The Henry Ford, "Origins of the Henry Ford," www.thehenryford.org/collections-and-research/digital-resources/popular-topics/origins-of-thf.

26. G.K. Chesterton, *A Short History of England* (New York: John Lane Co., 1917), 72.

27. Clifton Fadiman, *The Little, Brown Book of Anecdotes* (New York: Little, Brown, 1985), Kindle edition.

28. Daniel Edwin Wheeler, *Abraham Lincoln* (New York: Macmillan, 1916), 109.

29. Ibid., 108-9.

30. L. Tollemache, "Courage and Death," *The Fortnightly Review*, vol. 25, no. 109, January 1, 1876, 113. (A footnote reads, "This incident was mentioned in the House of Commons in 1873, and, I believe, purports to be authentic.") Some dialogue reconstructed for greater clarity.

31. Dave Anderson, "Sports of The Times; Marino and Shula's System," *New York Times*, November 4, 1984, www.nytimes.com/1984/11/04/sports/sports-of-the-times-marino-and-shula-s-system.html.

32. "Wesley to Wilberforce: John Wesley's Last Letter from His Deathbed," *Christian History*, www.christianitytoday.com/history/issues/issue-2/wesley-to-wilberforce.html.

33. FOXNews and Associated Press, "Satanic Temple Brings 'After School Satan Club' to Portland School," September 27, 2016, www.foxnews.com/us/2016/09/27/satanic-temple-brings-after-school-satan-club-to-portland-school.html.

34. Lenya Heitzig and Penny Rose, *Live Deeply: A Study in the Parables of Jesus* (Colorado Springs: David C. Cook, 2009), 208.

35. Michael Tanner, "The American Welfare State: How We Spend Nearly $1 Trillion a Year Fighting Poverty—and Fail," Policy Analysis No. 694, The Cato Institute, April 11, 2012, http://object.cato.org/sites/cato.org/files/pubs/pdf/PA694.pdf.

36. Ronald Reagan, *An American Life* (New York: Simon and Schuster, 1990), 68-69.

ABOUT THE AUTHOR

Michael Youssef, PhD, is the founder and president of Leading The Way, a worldwide ministry that leads the way for people living in spiritual darkness to discover the light of Christ through the creative use of media and on-the-ground ministry teams. His weekly television programs and daily radio programs are broadcast more than 4300 times per week in 25 languages to more than 190 countries. He is also the founding pastor of The Church of The Apostles in Atlanta, Georgia.

Dr. Youssef was born in Egypt and lived in Lebanon and Australia before coming to the United States. In 1984, he earned a PhD in social anthropology from Emory University. He and his wife reside in Atlanta and have four grown children and eight grandchildren.

For more on Michael Youssef, The Church of The Apostles, and Leading The Way, visit apostles.org and www.leadingtheway.org.

Other Harvest House Books by Michael Youssef

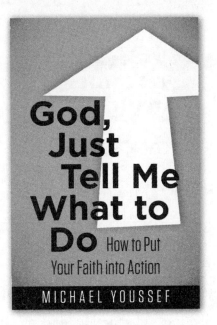

GOD, JUST TELL ME WHAT TO DO

God is constantly teaching us through our daily experiences. He wants us to master today's challenges and to be equipped to take on even greater challenges tomorrow.

In *God, Just Tell Me What to Do*, Michael Youssef offers biblical wisdom and encouragement to help you live out your Christian faith in such important areas as

- using your resources wisely
- thriving through trials and temptations
- understanding and obeying the Word of God
- guarding against the pressures of culture
- taming your tongue

Put your faith in action, and discover depths of strength, courage, and joy you never knew were waiting for you.

GOD, HELP ME OVERCOME MY CIRCUMSTANCES

We all go through seasons of struggle and testing. Regardless of our faith and our faithfulness to the Lord, adversity comes to us all.

In the Bible, God's people faced difficult circumstances as well, and nowhere is this seen more clearly than in the book of Judges. Drawing principles from this trying time in Israel's history, Michael Youssef helps us understand how the troubled seasons of our own lives lead to spiritual growth and maturity, and affirms that God's love is unfailing even in the midst of trials.

Discover how depending completely on God is the only response that never fails!

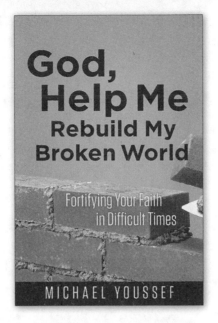

GOD, HELP ME REBUILD MY BROKEN WORLD

We live in a post-Christian age marked by moral and spiritual decay. We have watched our comfortable walls collapse as our faith has been attacked on every side.

But take heart—God can raise up people dedicated to defending His truth. And one of those people might be you, because no matter what your place in life, you have a circle of influence.

And your influence is desperately needed today.

How can you construct secure barriers to hold back the discouragement and moral danger of this world? Michael Youssef takes you through the book of Nehemiah to discover what it takes to rebuild walls in this highly relevant study of a people who traded their rubble for rejoicing.

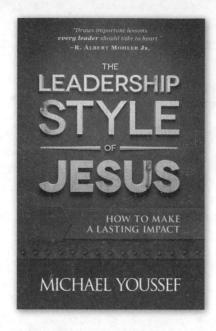

THE LEADERSHIP STYLE OF JESUS

Michael Youssef examines the leadership Jesus modeled and uncovers the Christlike qualities every leader needs, such as courage, gentleness, and truthfulness. But he doesn't stop there. With Jesus as the standard, Youssef considers how to deal with the temptations and pressures faced by a leader—such as loneliness, criticism, using power wisely, and passing the torch to others.

If you desire to excel in leadership, you'll find no better guide than this close-up look at Jesus—the greatest leader who ever lived.

To learn more about Harvest House books and
to read sample chapters, log on to our website:

www.harvesthousepublishers.com

HARVEST HOUSE PUBLISHERS
EUGENE, OREGON